EVASIVE PARADISE

PAUL ZEPPELIN

EVASIVE PARADISE

iUniverse books may be ordered through booksellers or by contacting:

iUniverse
1663 Liberty Drive
Bloomington, IN 47403
www.iuniverse.com
844-349-9409

ISBN: 978-1-6632-2740-9 (sc)
ISBN: 978-1-6632-2739-3 (e)

Print information available on the last page.

iUniverse rev. date: 08/04/2021

Foreword

In this new sixth book, Paul Zeppelin allows his rhymed verses to tenderly caress or even roughly plow every facet of human lives and our coexistence as such.

His wording is intriguing and magnetically captivating, challenging and demanding our full attention.

His poems are seamlessly structured so every word and its sound occupy a distinct location like in a stream of notes in a harmoniously and elegantly composed music.

This poet often lifts the curtain and lets us see our losses and gains, our failures and achievements.

A wonderful read.

Judith Parrish Broadbent
Author: *Golden Days: Stories and Poems of the Central South and Beyond.*

Am I still battling windmills?

Contents

The Windshield Views

The Windshield views
Run through these dazzling streets and avenues;
Only the rearview mirrors part our illusions from realities;
The nightmares from the brightest days of our dualities,
Or better yet, keep far apart our polar personalities.

Only the joy of glancing into evasive paradise
Squares with the cheery sunrays dancing on the melting ice,
Or better yet, the most unnerving chancing of the thrown dice;
Life is a gambling ticket. We pay the purchase price.

I Am its Singing Swan

I love the yachts of Monte Carlo,
The bright casinos in the harbor,
I see the shy Rachmaninoff,
Nicknamed a Russian Sable.
He keenly rakes his money off
The green cold-blooded table.

Feodor Chaliapin shatters glasses
With sounds of his mighty bass,
Anna Pavlova gracefully passes,
Wrapped in the filigree of lace.
The captivated idle masses
Catch glimpses of her veiled face.

I see the happy Isadora with Sergei
Already loaded in the light of day,
There are Picasso and Matisse,
Miss Baker doing her striptease,
Maestro Diaghilev runs his ballet,
Although, at night all cats are gray.

The cheery droves,
The lively beasts,
The days of bliss
Among the fauves,
The moving feasts
Of Russian émigrés.

The paradise of Monte Carlo,
Sparkly casinos in the harbor,
The silver epoch long has gone,
I stayed.
I am its singing swan.

I'm Alone Against the Sea

The starry sky already fell,
Only seagulls are left to scream,
Am I in Heaven or in Hell?
Or am I trapped in a silly dream?

I'm alone against the sea,
Like Hemingway's old man,
As tides of a sadistic glee
Rotate my dinghy like a fan.

Like a naughty hooligan,
Dawn sends down a breeze,
Now the moon is gone
And finally, I rest in peace.

A rapture for a jolly mind,
I jog my dead-beat boat,
The sails seem to have resigned
And only the stars can still float.

I think I'm a mighty oak,
My branches hug the sky,
I'm old; I can hardly walk,
Yet I still can pass you by.

I fan the flames
Of my illustrious days
Into lackluster nights
To cheer some names
That climb a staircase
Toward eternal lights.

It's time to stop and rest,
To take my life's inventory,
I try to do my very best,
To simply tell my story.

I Am Again a Boy

When I entertain the thoughts
Of my inevitable death,
Anticipating banned delights,
I'll no longer hold my breath,
I'll dive into my parting nights.

The dazzling nights,
The overwhelming joy,
Under the magic lights,
I'll become again a boy.

What's wrong with me?
I try, but can no longer bear
That quiet, unprotected glee
As my desire bouncily bursts,
Seeing the winds that dare
To lift the schoolgirls' skirts.

When I entertain the thoughts
Of my inevitable death,
I'll no longer hold my breath,
The good ones die so young,
Their songs remain unsung.

The closer I step towards
The end
Or rather, the grave,
The more I spend,
The less I save.

I'm like the other boys,
But with much better toys,
I pedal a Rolls Royce
And sail in my yacht,
I ride my horse,
They learn what I forgot,
Meanwhile, I carve a verse.

We live in the paradigm,
The spring has sprung.
It takes morbidity of my lifetime;
I turn my future on a dime.

I Am a Tribal Shaman

I am a tribal shaman,
I move to hell and back,
I am a rambling caveman
Far off the beaten track.

I always fight to win,
I search my soul,
I frisk my mind,
Remove the rainy clouds,
I dance the tango of a sin,
I reach my only goal
And leave behind
My scrambled doubts.

Those comedies will cry,
Those tragedies will laugh,
When I unveil the hidden lie
About diamonds in the rough.

I leave the nights of carnal joy,
I leave the days of fragile peace,
I am longing for the horse of Troy
To enter into a holy masterpiece.

I'm a Leaping Frog

Gray, unforgiving clouds
Swim in the moody skies
As medieval shrouds
Silence our futile cries.
They cloak the trees,
So nude without leaves,
Without fountains of gold,
So solitary and so cold.

The ice initiates its flow,
The spring comes soon,
I shut the door and go
To chirp under the moon.

I'm not a jumping dog,
I'm a happy leaping frog,
Across the morning blue
Into the diamonds of dew.

Though I'm in fine fettle,
It's not the time to settle,
It's frog-gigging season,
I hate you, Mother Nature,
I'll not forgive this treason,
This is my last adventure.

I'm a Horse

My life is almost over,
A pack of wolves encircled me
I'm petrified, but sober,
There is no time for poetry.

Their leader moves,
And now I must mention,
I'm but a horse,
I trudge my hooves.
Forgive my apprehension,
I'm scared to death, of course.

My master pulls his pistol,
I hear the bullet's whistle,
He glitters in his glory,
I live to tell the story.

I'm still a horse,
But now I am retired,
At times, I'd write a verse,
I dance and gulp my icy Bud.
Plus, when I'm not too tired,
I make some money as a stud.

I'm a Homeless Dreamer

I'm in Florence. Spring.
The cherries bloom,
The hearts of lovers sing,
The Sun comes to my room.

Grand Ponte Vecchio
Flaunts ancient arches
Reflected in the river;
Young lovers necking,
The crowd marches
Over the golden fever.

The city sculptures sprang
Into the nightly sky
Where all was blue before.
The raindrops rang,
The sparrows didn't fly,
The moon dozed on my floor.

A red sunset ran its bonfires
On silent, shoeless hoofs
Over the ancient orange tiles
Of always leaking roofs.

Young David looked at me,
The Captives tried to flee,
The glory of eternal marbles,
Veiled my neglected troubles.

The Brunelleschi Dome
Dressed in a sparkling red,
Loomed over the Arno River.
I heard, "Where are you from?"
I humbly said,
"I'm just a homeless dreamer."

I'll Share my Wine and Bread

I'll walk the graveyard of the living,
I'll walk the pasture of the dead,
I'll use the power of healing,
I'll share my wine and bread.

I'll see some honesty,
I'll hear the loud lies,
I'll see some modesty,
I'll hear the quiet cries.

The young girls grow,
The boys mature,
The seasons flow,
Tomorrows lure.

I'll walk into the warmth of sorrow,
I'll return into my cozy melancholy,
I'll postpone my joy until tomorrow,
I'll take pleasure in the prickly holly,
I'll wear the thorny winner's wreath,
As long as I can hear and breathe.

I'll Pay off My Debits

I'll acquire new habits,
I'll renounce my past,
I'll pay off my debits,
I'll go with a blast.

It is dusk; I lit the chandelier,
Two daughters joined the cast,
I am a caring gullible King Lear,
I am just a tourist from the past.

By early morning, I'll be gone,
The threshold sees my shadow,
My crown will be theirs at dawn,
The kingdom gets the afterglow.

What is in the name?
I am invited into bliss,
The solace of my fame
Gave me a farewell kiss.

Eternity will judge my life
And run it through a sieve.
Life is a cruel perpetual midwife,
She brings new days; we grieve.

I'll Die Without Blinders

Pierrot or Harlequin,
Clown or morbid kin;
I had to split myself in two,
It's not a parable; it's true;
It couldn't be much worse,
I'm not a man; I'm a horse.

Transgressions roll
The waterfall of sins,
I try to heal my soul,
I lose; nobody wins.

Too much is on my mind,
I write another verse,
I run through grinders,
The cruel verdict signed,
I'll die like a wild horse,
Without blinders.

My verse may die in vain,
Yet, it is not a futile fable;
I wrote a song of pain
For horses in the stable.

Too much is on my plate
Under the yoke of stress,
I run to the heaven's gate
To open them for horses
Before my passion crests,
Before I lose my verses.

I'd Rather Rob the Banks

I am an outsider on the flanks,
I am lost between the signs,
I'd rather rob the banks...
Why do I carve my lines?

At times, my rhymes,
My gloomy, shady verse,
Looks morbid or perverse.

Some faithfully serve Caesars,
Some praise their murky souls,
Some cut profiles with scissors,
Some even dance on the poles.
Some sow the seeds,
Some sign the deeds,
Some sign the wills,
Some take the pills.

Some only look, don't touch,
Is this too much?
Some only touch, don't taste,
Is this a waste?
Some only taste, don't swallow,
Is this too shallow?
Some only swallow, don't enjoy,
Is this a brutal ploy?

The greatest sin,
Is vanity of love;
Self-love, I mean.
A loveless dove

Will fight to win,
He wants to love.

A frozen sparkling teardrop
Fell from the leaded cloud,
My wisdom whispers "Stop,
Don't tear the Holy shroud,
The sun will heal the Earth;
We yet to celebrate rebirth,
We live life more than once,
Embrace the Renaissance."
An Empty Wineglass

All night 'til dawn
I heard the song
Of a dying swan,
The sound's piercing prong
Plagued me until he's gone.

After my futile body dies,
The beetles and the flies
Descend upon my flesh
As vultures on the trash.

The souls of faceless throngs
Wait on the untaken shelves,
But trusting rights and wrongs
Embrace the swarming elves.

I'll never see a rainbow
After that,
I craved a god sent glow,
Not a threat.

The darkest days will pass,
The nightmares disappear,
I hold an empty wineglass,
A witness of my drunken fear.

An Actor Leaves no Trace

Parisian nippy breeze
Brings fragile hopes,
Bends naked trees
Along the river slopes.

Bright rays of the limelight
Caress my vanity on stage,
After a curtain falls at night,
I feel no happiness or rage.

Same table,
Same café,
Same fable,
S'il vous plaît.

I like to work in France,
The land of royal lilies,
I am a mediocre actor,
Work makes no sense,
Tonight, I am Achilles,
Tomorrow, I am Hector.

I read the Judith's Book,
A tale of pseudo fairness,
I act again; I'm off the hook,
I'm a headless Holofernes.

At dusk, another play,
At dawn, another face,
Only the curtains sway,
An actor leaves no trace.

Am I a Predator or Prey?

Am I alive or dead?
Am I a needle or a thread?
Am I a predator or prey?
Do I direct or just obey?

I'm on the ship of fools,
I wonder if I'll ever dock,
I often trail the mothballed rules,
Carved on the Plymouth Rock.

I run from the nights of darkness
Toward the days that disappear,
Our world is relatively heartless,
Although, I'm still breathing here.

The stars don't warm me anymore,
They only swirl above and wink,
The Bible-thumpers pledge a war,
The skeptics lose before they blink.

I daily check the Heavens' signs,
But never trail obscure advises,
I simply read between the lines
And pick my truths, but check
The prices.

Along a Flawed Delight

The judgment of Paris,
The fruit of contention,
Take it or leave it,
Be sharp and swift.
I thank you, Botticelli,
For this amazing gift:
Three optimistic graces
Wait for the Grand Prix,
But only La Primavera,
The gorgeous spring,
The alpha and omega
In a rebirth of anything,
Pauses their rivalry
And vicious tension...

I'm not a god; I'm free,
Nobody turns my meal,
It's not a steering wheel
On a half-finished plate.
Nobody pedals my canoe,
I won't enjoy the gait,
It's not a pas de deux.

Nobody reigns over my life,
It's simply black and white,
Pure as a morning dew.
In my own view,
I learned to live and thrive
Along a flawed delight.

I crossed the threshold
Of God's eternal ploy,
I'm sure. He wants to fold
His quest for love and joy.

The tender, loving doves
May never cross the sky.
Our unanswered loves
Bare pains, yet never cry.

Along a Dotted Line

Illusions disappear,
Footprints evaporate,
Only a salty, sticky fear
Reminds me of my fate.

Sometimes, I fly,
Sometimes, I crawl,
I often aim too high,
I will inevitably fall.

I tear the rite of spring,
Along a dotted line,
Today, life pours a drink,
I'm ready to resign.

I daily wear in vain
A straight jacket
Of your love,
I cry, I am in pain,
Stroked by a velvet hand
In an iron glove.

I earn a day of peace,
You are a nasty dream,
A phantom of the night,
A penetrating breeze,
A petrifying scream,
A devastating fight.

You will remember me.
We'll never meet again,
I leave you in your glee,
While I'm still insane.

A tarnished cross
Hangs on my chest,
My angel hovers close,
I am a host,
He's an uninvited guest.

Aloneness is a Gift

Aloneness is a gift
From His high-minded boredom;
Only His penalties and treats,
Only His sunsets' bloody sheets,
Above St. Peter's hollow dome
Give Lucifer a necessary lift.

My fears are lain
Like heavy boulders
On my guilt-ridden soul;
Like a long-lasting pain
Across my shoulders,
While life is dancing
Naked on the pole.

Blind Homer wrote concisely
About our shattered hearts,
About Cupid's loving darts,
Piercing them so precisely
That life still imitates the arts.

Our prophets exposed God
As innocently pure role model,
They didn't see the lightning rod;
His son who loved to mollycoddle
The sick, the hungry and the meek,
Ignored all those who reach the peak.

Life drowns us in our own confusions,
And yet, we're the masters of illusions,
Virtues are ignored; vice is rewarded,
But only innocence gets water-boarded.

Almighty or Big Bang

Charles Darwin's intuition
Derived from many pools,
His motto of the mission,
"Evolution rules!"

That's all there is,
Abandoned thrones,
An eternity of freeze,
The piercing thorns
Cut into elastic souls
Of blind believers,
Into the misty goals
Of keen achievers.

One night, I drank alone,
Eureka feverously rang,
I heard it on the phone,
"I started with the Bang."

A touch of evolution,
A splinter of creation,
It is my contribution
To our weird elation.

What's in a name?
Instead of pride or fame,
Choose your own slang,
Almighty or Big Bang.

Allow Me the Pain of Love

I take the road shoulder,
And hustle to my flight,
I'm getting really bolder,
I'm looking for a fight.

I leave my yesterdays
To fly across the skies
And watch new days
In your beloved eyes.

My mother cuts the cord,
I lose my comfort blanket,
I offer you my world,
You took and banked it.

The moon hums a lullaby
To sorrows on your face,
Don't move, stand by,
I crave to kiss that lace.

I have to take my losses,
I can't rerun the past,
I hold a bouquet of roses,
But its petals fall too fast.

Look in my eyes,
They cheat no more,
Clear as the skies
Above a sunny shore.

You suffered long enough
Edged by the burning trees,
Allow me the pain of love,
I beg you; I'm on my knees.

All Others Missed

My rhymes cast shadows
Without the honey scent
Of happiness within them.
I see no colors of delight,
I see no arcs of rainbows
Across a highway bend,
Just silence of the lamb
Above a trembling light.

You saw, all others missed
My verses' filigree,
They weren't ever kissed,
They're tone-deaf to our glee.

Trees shed each leaf,
As you shed your silky dress,
You stand like Adam's Eve
And softly whisper, "yes."

You generously give me
A heaven of sapphires,
Malachite of grass,
The waves of a stormy sea,
The sunsets' burning fires,
And autumn's shiny brass.

We're the same pages
In the scrolls of souls,
The tombs of sages
Seal our hollow goals.

Alexandra, My Grandma

My granny's in her armchair on the porch,
So regal in the shade of her beloved birch,
She glanced at me; I caught her glance
And jumped into the saddle from the fence.

I loved to ride my flirty horse,
She was so smart and gentle,
Never capricious, never coarse,
I keep her picture on my mantel.

The image of a cavalcade all in the pinks,
Ahead, enthusiastic hounds running fast.
The cozy memories of these chain links
Connect me with the forever vanished past.

My granny Alexandra liked her name
After the prophetess of a Trojan fame,
Who could foresee reality from fiction,
But no one trusted her prediction.

"Grandma,
Why in your eyes I see a silent scream,
Yet when we talk, they spark and beam?"
"You're still a boy; but you must understand,
I'm concerned about your challenges ahead.
You'll be a man: walk straight, don't ever bend,
You may lose a precious crown on your head."

Under her birch grandma was laid to rest,
I'm in the saddle of my lifelong quest…

Again, a Rearview Mirror

Touched by a tender dawn,
The beach is veiled by dunes,
My loving grandma gone,
A wind brings dusted tunes
To her great country house.
I'm back, I have returned,
I guess, I'm a second mouse.
I got what I haven't earned.

Again, a rearview mirror,
My past seems clearer,
I've been mistreated,
I've been abused,
Never well greeted,
Frequently confused.

I reached the edges
Of myself,
Beyond those futile pledges
Waiting on the dusty shelf.

I have reentered my own skin,
I went to justify my own existence,
But every friend and every kin
Stood indifferently still.
I walked alone that distance.

Midnight, I'm sitting on the floor,
Listening to my life's complaints,
Someone's knocking on my door,
I wonder who is there,

My losses or my gains?
I pulled a shotgun, aimed
And welcomed to come in.
My memory flashed red, ashamed,
For there stood a gentle harlequin.

Long live the tragedy of a comic art,
Our masked recollections a la carte.

After the Rain

I thanked you for a lovely dinner
With comfortable rituals of grace,
I didn't hide my true demeanor
Under the mask of a happy face.

The quest is higher than my goal,
I want to learn its hidden meaning,
My Lord, I'll hock my trembling soul
If you display the world's beginning.

He said, "There was a word,
I heard cacophonies of silent nights
About seven days of a real patience,
But then the most unpleasant sights
Of my inept and talentless creations.
And yet, I made this world,
Some sorrows turned into my joy,
Few joys turned into my sorrows,
Your melancholy won't destroy
My expectations for tomorrows.

My verdict has been signed,
The days and nights aligned,
After the rain's straight lines
A rainbow bends and shines.

I gave you seven jolly colors,
You live with seven fatal sins,
I let you gamble a few dollars,

But when the final trial begins,
A gambler borrows,
But the lender wins."

I risked my shaking soul,
He didn't reach his goal.

After the Guns

I touched his ashen face,
His eyes that failed to see
Les Mortes graines d'amour.
The bullets in this race,
The lifeless seeds of love,
Fly to the gates of glee
That shimmer far above
This endless fruitless war.

After the guns
Have fallen silent,
The blood still runs,
The sorry notes got sent,
The starry flags got folded.
Warmongers never scolded.

White angels
And black ravens
Betrayed us all.
They stole the keys
And locked safe havens
From every wounded soul,
From visions of tomorrows
Without wars and sorrows.

The dreams recede,
The hopes advance.
Both seed and feed
Our foes and friends.

Farewell, the past,
Life is for the living,
The wars won't last
When we are willing.

Autumn Leaves

Her take-it-or-leave-it invitation,
Brings me into the blinding light,
I'm a train that left its station
For a better-than-expected night.

A fragile dawn, an early hour,
A slice of French baguette,
A cup of bitter Earl gray tea,
My girlfriend takes a shower,
I smoke my morning cigarette,
A suicidal Pall Mall, filter free.

She won't even bother
To tell her mother
That she is happy in my bed.
Until last night, she was misled
By the gray-haired traditions
About saving a virgin cherry
Till the bridal night's auditions.

I whisper, "Don't marry
If you can't stand the heat,
But losing your sweet cherry
Is just a memorable treat."

The sun paints the fluffy clouds,
Dead-end ideas lose, time wins,
Dismissing nights of futile doubts.

I haven't seen that beauty since.

The golden autumn leaves
Descend onto my shoulders,
My heavy heart still grieves
In vain, as Sisyphus' boulders.

Time wins.

A Pear-Shaped Teardrop

After wet dreams of every teen,
We lived in carnivals of clowns
Without middlemen between
The dinners and restrooms,
Between the wedding gowns
And thrusting pimpled grooms.

Today, I'm sun-tanned and shaven,
Wearing a self-indulging wreath.
I'm astute as a tempered raven,
Above the fray, seldom beneath.
I have my own distinguished style,
New trends arrive and disappear,
Two hands still moving on the dial
Toward a thought-provoking year.

If it's too lonely at the top,
A pear-shaped teardrop
Finds its wrinkle-riverbed
And slowly moves ahead
In search of vivid colors
Dividing bravery and fear
Amid the foes and lovers
Struggling far and near.

Kaleidoscopes of flowerpots
On balconies of solitary widows
Resembled shattered thoughts
Of dusty stained-glass windows.

The lightning stroked the clouds,
The thunders played the drums,
The raindrops swept my doubts
Like a few weather-beaten mums.

Caveat emptor was presumed,
Nevertheless, I lost my faith,
And blamed no one.
The lies were well perfumed,
Life didn't have to bathe
And didn't hide its smoking gun.

A Path into The World Divine

I'm grazing freely
Through my early verses,
Revisiting my past
And harvesting flashbacks.
I'm still a shaded outcast
With pain and controversies,
Yet, happy in my tracks.

In my pursuit of the beginning,
I run or swim against the flow,
The underdogs are winning,
When top dogs start to glow.

I'm in pursuit of virtues
In prehistoric people
And in my distant brother.
Predictably, my searches
Led me to a single mother,
A foremost, epicentral nipple.

I even dove into the deep
In search of a paradigm,
I didn't see a worthy yield
To reap,
Just lost some costly time.

I'm rudely asked to pay a lot
For my unfortunate mistakes,
I didn't slash the Gordian knot
I didn't bang on rusty brakes.

I'm just loaded with my flaws.
I didn't sink; I hung on straws.

I would prefer a softer turn,
A glass of luscious wine,
I lived, but failed to earn
A path into the world divine.

There is no other way,
There is a price I didn't pay.

A Pact

Tall golden-crowned maples
Border my stamp-sized yard,
I listen to sweet oldies-staples
Like a thick-skinned die-hard.

Help me through the day
And leave me for tonight,
I'll dream of my tomorrows
As if my life is a magic play.
I hope to hear, "let it be light"
And see the end of sorrows.

What have I done?
Do I deserve my luck?
Am I the only one
Who effortlessly struck
A pact with all my saints
To live with no restraints.

I never argue with my fate,
Today, I'm silly sloshed
And stand before the gate.
My sins are washed,
They were wrung dry
With someone's final cry.

Life was a path of lies
Into the field of truth.
The sun must always rise
Into the innocence of youth.

A Noxious Doubt

I swim against the current,
Although, I realize,
I won't get out
Of this life alive.
The stage of life is curtained,
So death won't enter in disguise.
I send away my noxious doubt
About real winners in this strive.

I'm fighting tooth and nail,
But if I slide to the abyss,
I pledge, I'll never miss
The splendor of the golden age,
The black or white tie parties,
The girls primped head to toes,
The strutting peacocked gents
Wooing the girls with pigeon chests,
Bleached hairs and plastered faces.
I'd like to turn that page,
Forget those brainless babies,
Those striking robots wearing clothes,
Looking for gold over the fences,
Blindly ignoring all the other quests
That lose all other races.

But I'll miss the sun,
Above the fields and seas,
I'll miss my loyal dogs,
I'll miss my birds and horses,
I'll miss my tender dawn
Above the flowers and the trees,

I'll miss my clumsy blogs
Spewing my candid verses.

Regrettably, I'll lose this strive,
I won't get out of this life alive.

A Nightingale

The sphinx sincerely mourns,
Touched by your quiet song,
My gold-tongued nightingale.
Beneath the crescent horns
The nights are hot and long
Like this pearl-studded tale.

Your voice flies like a dove,
Show me your face, unveil,
I want to hug my tender love,
I want to kiss my nightingale.

You are my gorgeous girl,
My unexpected love affair,
You are my precious pearl,
My gentle nightingale.

Cathedrals gleam at night
For those who soar or fail,
The angels fly in sight
To hear you, Nightingale.

Across the purling stream
Of a never-ending dream,
I reached the Holy Grail,
I kissed you, nightingale.

Along the gothic naves
We sail the seas of truth,
We sing above the graves
Of innocence and youth.

A Never-Ending Glee

I stood terribly sad and cold
On rocks above a river bend,
You pushed; I fell and rolled
Toward our love's dead-end.

My calendar turned many pages
With empty squares of lazy days,
Like silent, never-lived-in-rooms,
Totally sheltered from the rages
Of modern spectacles and plays,
Marching amid forgotten tombs.

I'm coming back; it was enough,
I'm a dove returning to my love.
To climb the knowledge tree
And carve "Love equals glee".

The worn-out snow will melt soon,
You'll find my letters tossed away,
You'll walk under a floating moon
Among the shades of love in play.

You're drained by someone else,
Yet I'm sure, there's a sip for me,
My gut-wrenched intuition tells,
You are my never-ending glee.

Even if you're kind and clever,
Love can't survive unbruised,

Love guards its days insanely,
Sometimes too cold and rainy,
Love flaunts its scars forever
And keeps us utterly confused.

A Moral Arrogance of Faith

I place a fancy garnish
Lengthwise the Bible's songs,
It's just a see-through varnish
For my religious wrongs.

A moral arrogance of faith
Spins like a merciless lathe.

My head is waiting on the tray,
Surrounded with dancing goons,
The strings of my tormented soul
Can't any longer bear this play,
I want to hear the ancient tunes,
I want to read the earliest scroll.

My tortured soul screams,
"Don't help me through the day,
Just help me through the night."
Don't kill my fragile dreams,
They used to fly above the fray
And glowed in their blinding light.
It is too late. I hear the bell,
It was my fate. The curtain fell.

They'll forgive me once or twice,
They'll be reasonable and wise,
They'll use integrity and rhymes,
They'll punish me without crimes.

I push my glut of luck,
I waste my time in vain,
I try to pass the buck,
But I'm the one to blame.

I promise not to use
My dogmas' crushing flood,
I promise not to use
A moral arrogance of faith,
The river of my blood
Is not for you to bathe.

A Mistake

I watch my quiet street
Through a parted curtain,
The kids guess trick-or-treat,
But our fates remain uncertain.

Even the gentle angels cry,
Listening to my old story,
In vain, I feverishly try
To climb a wall of worry.

Their all-forgiving hearts
Lent me its darker side,
I've learned the futile arts
Of envy, vanity and pride.

Blue heavens said goodbye,
White winter chilled my soul,
Red cardinals refused to fly,
We always play a fated role,
A fallen angel flew without me,
I flew to the abyss,
He flew to glee.

We're all actors, we're weak,
We're exposed to a mistake,
Since all the world's a stage.
Some give, some only take,
Some turn the other cheek,
I simply write another page.

A Melting Pot

We all are
Equal in a melting pot of trenches,
Away and far
From comfortable park benches,
From politics and our religions,
From our go-get-them drives,
From our pseudo patriotic lieges,
From lives in a melting pot of lies.

We learn the sweaty fear of death,
We learn to love, to hate and cry,
We learn to fight till our final breath,
We learn to sigh when brothers die.

I'm ready at the window seat,
The helicopter petals-fans
Make a rhythmical drumbeat.
I see no volunteers to dance.
Sun rolls above the ridge,
The river whips its banks
And runs under the bridge.
I only hear the roaring tanks.

Another scorching afternoon,
Our lieutenant led the siege,
The bullets sang a deadly tune,
We left behind a blown bridge.

We left behind that score,
We kept the stars and bars,
We left behind that war,

We left behind our fears,
We brought on us the scars,
We left behind our peers.

We're back together,
We're back to our melting pot,
We're still guessing whether
Our country loves or loves us not.

A Master of a Metaphor

I'm a reverend,
I came from the abyss,
I'm irrelevant
To wars in earthly bliss,
I'm an uninvited infant,
I'm an unwelcomed kiss.

I like the old routine
Of betting in casinos,
A dime to enter,
A buck to leave.
I'm floating between
Merlots and pinots,
I'm a cheerful lamenter
With aces in my sleeve.

The chase is thrilling,
I run a high-stakes table,
At night all cats seem gray,
I'm definitely willing,
But hardly ever able
To pick a predator or prey.

A leading master of a metaphor
Once said: "It has been known
What you're fighting for,
You'll reap what has been sown.
Those who pursue perfection
Will live long lives, but die alone.
You'll wear a crown of rejection,
Descending from your throne."

Gods don't forget the dead,
Only the living get forgotten,
I'm still hanging on a thread,
That's all what I have gotten.

A Masquerade of Souls

Our virtues stay in perils
Without honorable goals,
Life turns into the empty
Barrels,
Into a futile masquerade
Of souls.

Life is a rapid game,
There are few blinks
Between the diapers
And the chill of graves.
When our future sinks,
A legal clerk deciphers
Matters, no one craves.

Masks cover baffled souls,
Hide morbid gaudy trends
Amid the guarding poles
Of enemies and friends.

There's a tiny ray of hope,
Desires may seize the day,
Our fate becomes a dope,
Our life becomes a fray.

Despite a daily prose
That silently adjourns,
There is no purpose
Besides the art of life,
The beauty of a rose
And cruelty of thorns.

Our virtues stay in perils
Without honorable goals,
Life turns into an empty
Barrels,
Into a futile masquerade
Of souls.

.

A Marble Faun

A burial ground,
A marble faun
Plays in a shade,
He is glee bound,
As an early dawn
Came as his date.

The costly diamonds of dew
Fall from a tender cloud,
The birds are very few,
Yet cheerfully loud.

The means don't justify the ends,
My scars already know the truth,
I miss my enemies and friends,
I miss the troubles of my youth.

I'm revisiting my past,
The old familiar rules,
The skies are overcast
Above a ship of fools.

I see no crosses or any stars
Above the nameless graves,
Only the tarnished metal bars
Protect the fallen braves.

Again, it's cold,
Again, there's rain,
I'm cowardly, not bold,
I miss the train called Life,

It's killing me, it's all in vain,
It gives me nothing in return,
I'm wrapped in silence
Of ill-considered reasons,
I live and feverishly learn,
Why life neglects its seasons.

I practice my idiosyncratic habit,
My tall hat hides a pretty rabbit,
Give me a chance and I'll bring
The gentle innocence of spring.

A Map is never a Terrain

A ritual of distrust,
Dismissed illusions,
A stoic discontent,
Presumptuous lust
Of our futile fusions,
All under a tiny tent.

A map is never a terrain,
The world fell in my lap,
Under the strings of rain,
Life may become a trap.

Too many losses to forget,
Too many tears to wipe,
Too many roads to walk,
Too many errors to regret,
Too many words to type,
Too many souls to cloak.

Too many ills to grieve,
Too little time to love,
Too many lies to sieve,
Too little truth above.

I try to hone my dart,
I try to walk upstream,
I try to heal my heart,
I try to live my dream.

I had to learn a lot to be a child,
To simplify my life through knowledge,

To escape banalities and emptiness
Of provincial life.
Last night, I looked in the mirror
And recognized myself
In that learned man.
I welcomed my tomorrows,
Life's death without them.

A Man of Solitude

We ran without shadows
Like ripples on the lakes,
We climbed the gallows
To hang our weary aches.

We were the graveyards
For the wedding cakes,
We "blistered" our cards,
We sold our painted fakes.

We ran our dusted DNA's
Through labyrinths of lies,
We knew the Q's and A's
Before we'd cast the dice,
We carved our verses
With pain and curses.

We sailed the seas of war,
We saw these films before.

The years of innocence,
The gold of leafy showers,
The silver strings of rain,
The loud urban nuisance,
The endless happy hours.
I wonder if I am still sane.

I'm grateful for blindness,
I still can't watch the tears,
I'm grateful for brightness
Of these remaining years.

These days, I live a quiet life,
Nobody is around to intrude,
No one is longing for a strife,
I'm a man of solitude.

A Man of Faith

I'm in the crosshairs
Of streets and avenues,
I'm the one who cares,
The one who will refuse
To write new verses
As a ticking paradox
Of the unrhythmic clocks.

My verse is just a guide
That opens hidden doors
From principals of youth
Into obscurity of truth.

Lampoonery and flaunting
Of Eden's fruitless wisdom tree,
Borders the merciless taunting
Of human skinless sensitivity.
I regularly fret and fume
Ignored, abused and stupid,
Abandoned in a waiting room
To entertain already convoluted.

I juggled lines and rhymed
When my intuition climbed
The barren wisdom tree and fell
Too far from heaven,
Too close to hell.

My fragile conscience
Answers questions
That weren't ever asked,

It brings to light my anxious
Carriers of dire intentions
Concealed and masked.

Religion is a turning lathe
Enhancing timid dogmas
For our Sunday schools.
Though, I'm a man of faith
In many other wilted rules,
Estranged from our sterile
Ten commandments.

A Lunatic at Large

In my obscure salacious dreams,
I watched my error-strewn days,
A floor was higher than a ceiling,
I've swum against the streams,
Avoiding odious displays
Of gluttony among the willing.

I didn't have a wink of sleep,
I left my partners in the dust,
It was the saddest leap,
But I'll repeat it if I must.

While I was hooting in the dark,
My angel stretched his wings
And soared, all of a sudden,
Above the rainbow arc.
Among few precious things,
He left for me the magic lamp
Of a magnanimous Aladdin.

From now on, I enter
Many doors without keys,
And always say the same
In every nightly prayer:
"I'm not a meek lamenter,
I blissfully sway on a trapeze,
Above a scorching flame,
I'm not a loser, I'm still a payer."

My kindness went to rest,
My wickedness erupted,

My creativity confessed,
I used few rhymes abducted.

I'm a provider of dead souls
To our planetary neighbors,
I read to them the Holy scrolls
Surrounded by rattling sabers.
I'm a knife-wielding lunatic at large,
Even the night guards of the abyss
Demand from me a cover charge.

A Lull Before the Storm

A lull before the storm,
I pull my navy uniform,
Just one more sin,
A single battle left,
It will be hard to win,
I'm old, no longer deft.
A lull before the storm,
I pulled my uniform.

War shakes the world,
War ruins soldiery lives,
War starts before a word,
War only in a myth is wise.

Smoke lifts upwards
Into the starry skies,
A village falls asleep,
I try to weave the words,
I couldn't close my eyes,
My soul began to weep.

A wounded heart brings
Lonely nights,
A broken mirror brings
Sorrows of the past.
I hope to see the lights
Over a quilt of overcast.

My fate,
A lull before the storm,
Too late,
I pawned my uniform.

A Lifetime Yoke

My mother's Day of birth,
Midnight, Times Square,
A New Year's Eve,
A crystal planet Earth.
As always,
Something new to wear,
As always,
Resolutions to achieve.

I found an asylum
For my rhymes,
Between two signs of
Stop and Yield,
Expecting punishments
For crimes
Of my inborn intelligence
Concealed.

My tenderizing fret,
My disconcerted fears,
Arrested my desires to bet
Against the loyalty of peers.

When hope was hanging
On a thread,
I didn't write my verses
For the dead,
Only obituaries sealed
My buddies on a battlefield.

Thin curling stream
Of aimless smoke
Escapes a naked chimney
Like a determined thread
That pays my lifetime yoke
Of a never shrinking debt
To those who never knew
God's daily bread.

A Lifelong Banquet

Red rose's fallen petals
Covered the ground
Like our patriotic rebels
Forever Dixie bound.

Sunset turns bloody red,
They dump their chains
And gallop straight ahead
Tightly adjusting reins
They had no lives to waste,
They had no other cheeks
To turn,
They only had their future
To foretaste,
They had the final bridge
To burn.

Singing their father's song,
They jumped into the night,
I wasn't there to sing along,
I had the other wars to fight.

Behind a heavy smoke,
A blue-eyed sloppiness
Of these light-minded folk
Turned into a total mess.
They play a game
Of ducks and drakes

And calmly claim
A weightless blanket
Of sparkly snowflakes
For a lifetime banquet.

A Lewd Seductress

The days of laughs
Bring nights of tears,
Her moody roughs
Turn off the cheers.

She is a lewd seductress,
She is a boisterous night,
She is a flirtatious actress
She is a winner in this fight.

She plucks and picks
Evasive birds of happiness,
The aimless strangers
On the streets of sorrows,
The lonesome freaks,
The joyful nights and days,
The wingless angels,
The darkness of tomorrows.

She has discovered our souls
As virgin, never acted roles,
Veiled in the Dead Sea scrolls,
Until the curtain falls.

A Letter to Pegasus

So many years are passing by
Like hordes of life's marauders,
The heavens desperately sigh,
Then stamp our patient waters,
Forgiving seven sins, we own
And reaping what we've sown.

I'll never write much better,
I cannot write much worse,
I'm writing a conciliatory letter
To a goodhearted flying horse.

A rising evenhanded tide
Will generously lift all boats.
My boat will take me for a ride
Along the river that still floats
Between the lies and justice,
Between abuse and fairness,
Between insanity and sense,
Between astute and careless.

I dodged a "yes" or "no" fork
Of our hostilities' quicksand
Under a vicious overcast
Of syrupy retaliations.
I simply chose a wedding band,
With hope that peace will last
Under the rays of vindications,
Under a sign "goodwill at work".

As horses with the blinds,
We run into the walls,
Of our tortured minds
And dedicated goals.

I run from my despair
Toward the land of glee,
I loathe to breathe the air
Polluted by eternal misery

A Letter Home

Dear Mom,
This is a heartfelt letter
From your unruly debtor.
My thoughts don't come
From dreams about peace,
From dreams about mirth.
They come
From the infinity of freeze,
And from the hell on Earth.

The awful war,
The march of death,
The flying slugs…
I'm scared and sore,
I hold my breath,
I miss your hugs.

Under the foreign sky
Rain dribbles by my face,
I hear the missiles fly
And whisper sacred grace.

I was just now christened,
A god of war was flawless,
The angry bullets glistened
Across this bleeding mess.

My bosom buddy fell,
Their sniper didn't miss,
I mumbled: "War is hell,
Goddamn beheaded bliss."

This war will never end,
It is a river of eternal fear,
The Satan held that hand,
Which sent us to die here.

Dear Mom,
This is my final letter
I'm your eternal debtor.

A Wavy River of Your Hair

A wavy river in your hair,
The ocean in your eyes,
Anticipation of your flare.
I wonder how many tries
The gentle angels hated
Before you were created.

Your gorgeous face
Resembles madness
Of the dancing nights
Tearing the silky lace
Of our daily sadness
Wrapped in the lights.

I loved
'til dusks abandoned lights,
I loved
'til silence choked the nights,
I loved
'til hopes embraced the past,
I loved
'til sunny rays blew overcast,
I loved
'til lovely angels rang the bell,
I loved
'til vicious devils cast the spell.

I'll sail the sea of time,
I'll cross the spread,

I'll chuck the dime,
I'll steal or earn,
I'll look ahead,
I shall return.

A Vivid Flowerbed of Endless Love

A vivid flowerbed of endless love,
A mighty magnet of eager souls,
The one I was still dreaming of,
While hiding in the rabbit holes.

I outlived my yearnings' zest,
I blame a headache when I fail,
My girlfriend strokes my chest
Like poetry inscribed in Braille.

Behind a mask of hippie-bangles
I hide a shameful dementia galore,
My mind only rejects or tangles,
But can no longer keep the score.

I move ahead by leaps and bounds
Sideways my grossly deviated fate,
Between the hordes of outliers,
And hardly keep my wobbly footing.
While making rather futile rounds,
I realized it's probably too late
To turn the other cheek to liars
Or stop my loyal friends from looting
The tarnished and yet priceless gold
Of gaudy images and joints I rolled,
From verses of my burlesque role,
From hidden treasures of my soul,
Which they don't know, I have sold,
They missed. Gods broke the mold.

A Vessel of Remorse

A brutal stranger,
A wingless angel
Ascended from a fire
Into my life's quagmire.

Nevertheless, he spoke,
Ill-mannered, senseless.
I stood entirely friendless,
Draped in a guilty smoke
Amid my unforgiven sins,
That's how the end begins.

Don't soothe my pain
It strides its course.
I'm not a moving train,
I'm a boat without oars.

A paradise can wait
Don't heal my soul,
Please, stay awhile,
I'll camouflage my fate,
I'll play my parting role,
I'll dance my extra mile.

I'll be a vessel of remorse
Amid the wrong and right,
Sailing in the sea of pain,
Writing my humble verse
Rhyming the rays of light
With teardrops of the rain.

A Puzzle Landed on My Plate

Back from a morning stroll,
I microwaved a hefty bowl
Of good old cheesy grits
To energize my sleepy wits.

A puzzle landed on my plate,
I asked my cultivated friend,
Please, solve a riddle. I'll wait.
I wonder if it has a happy end.

I bet, gods penned it far above
Of ancient snow-dusted roofs,
And laid into effect their love,
Creating us to live like wolves.

Twigs break, trees only bend,
We run away if we can't fight
Or join the winners for a while.
Even the darkest tunnels end,
And we enjoy the blinding light
Above the treasures of the isle.

Here's gods' puzzle-inquisition,
"Tell us, what's your position,
Is life a happy journey for a one
Or a lifelong brutal competition?"
I said, "Uncertainty has gone,
Life was, still is and will remain
The most malicious competition.
You shaped us as the wolves,
We're not gentle, loving doves,

We watch each other's moves,
Ready to fight with iron gloves.
We live like boxers in the ring
We win or get knocked down.

For each of us may be the king,
But only one will wear the crown."

A Quiet Confession

Even the longest threads must end,
Only the valleys never rise,
Only the hills never descend.
Love is a beating heart of happiness,
Love is a shuttle between no and yes,
Love can't be holy and eternal,
It stays capricious and nocturnal.

Times roll on the shiny rails
Of my nostalgic myths,
Stop, sleep, wake up,
Move backward or ahead,
The future morphs into a broken cup,
Reminding me of our unwanted gifts,
Instead of an anticipated daily bread.

The sun burns both criminals and saints,
Yet neither party files complaints,
Only the lumps of nightly darkness
Still hiding in the muddy ditches
And turning off the switches
Of woken hopes and sleepy lightness.

A delicious poured wine has to be drunk,
Somebody's treasure is someone's junk,
It's our colorless wallpaper of existence,
We often walk the path of least resistance,
These days, one must be quiet to be heard,
If we start a riot, we kill the singing bird.

We lose the warmth of our souls
If deaths arrive without invitations,
We even read the Dead Sea scrolls,
Our trains are leaving their own stations.

Abandoned Rocky Trail

Abandoned rocky trail,
The river dried in vain,
I am a boat without a sail,
A car over the yellow line

Pour to the golden rim,
I'm your old and tired friend,
I'm weed that needs a trim,
I've sinned; I won't ascend.

I've been to paradise.
I drank Champagne
Until I closed my eyes,
I saw infinity in pain,

I'm a lonely ship
Still rocking on the wave
I never stopped to sip,
I'm getting rather brave.

La Vie en rose,
Discards the sorrows,
My poetry is like a prose,
It never sees tomorrows.

A Young Firefighter

I'm a new firefighter-volunteer,
The house is wrapped in flames,
I hardly manage all that gear
And water hoses' heavy chains,
The smoke is rising to the skies,
But fire still dances in my eyes.

This happened many years ago
Under the moon's unending flow,
That fire forever changed my life,
One of the saved is still my wife.

A Winner Dies Alone

I don't expect
A miracle from fate,
My saints protect
My heart from hate.

A shotgun barrel,
The last resort,
The ending peril
Fell overboard.

No one yet won,
A loser will be loved,
A winner dies alone,
Truth will be shoved.

A blessing in disguise,
Our history is changed,
A revolution in the skies,
A fallen Lucifer avenged.

White tender clouds
Float our souls and fates
Across the sea of doubts,
While heaven waits.

A Wingless Angel

I try to organize my world
As if I'm a director of the plays,
And search for the primal word.
The dancers sing in my ballets.

Life is my theatre of the absurd,
I see it through a dusty window,
In front of me a clumsy ugly bird,
A longnecked pink flamingo.

I'm infatuated with the birds,
Folks don't intrigue me anymore,
I know them, just mark my words,
They crawl and never want to soar.

My morbid dreams came to fruition,
A wingless angel found the ignition,
My starship kissed goodbye the Earth,
Hello, the Renaissance. Hello, Rebirth.

A Lasting Truce

I long for beauty of perfection,
I long for kindness of the sun,
I long for Calliope's affection,
Hot as a smoking gun.

My wasteful attempts
To reach a lasting truce,
Between aggressive pages
Of my book,
Told me, "No one should lose,
Each one desires a cozy nook".

My pun-free, true-life verses
Run as yet unsaddled horses,
We touch the iron fist of law,
Before we see its tragic flaw.

I was a hound and a finder,
My Calliope was not a keeper,
My poetry escaped the binder,
Caught, skinned and boned,
Then fed into a cruel grinder,
All rhymes were captured,
Rearranged, reshaped, reread,
Then brought into the rapture

I'm a finder of my muse,
I'm her unwilling keeper,

I gratefully take her views
Or humbly dig much deeper,
I long for beauty of perfection,
I long for Calliope's affection.

A La Carte

I didn't have to read the scroll,
The callous time has stopped,
I couldn't get the leading role,
The final curtain dropped.

I used to drink your love,
You were my morning dew.
I loved; I was a loving dove,
In love, infinity is often blue.
We danced, I could foresee,
The end of our Pas de deux.

These days, I dance alone
The tango of a broken heart
Toward my graveyard stone,
Into the final menu a la carte.

The autumn flaunts its gold,
The winter vows at the door,
Without you I am already cold,
Awaiting the Apocalyptic Four.

A Jewish Fiddler

Under the dome of a cathedral
The flames of candles shiver
Next to a gentle Jewish fiddler,
Whose music flows like a river.

The sounds of his fiddle
As pure as a loving dove,
A crying enigmatic riddle,
No one yet tried to solve.

I left behind those breezy years,
I grabbed my youth war-bound,
And left behind my sweaty fears,
But took to war his dreamy sound.

Though wounded, I returned,
War rudely changed our lives,
I looked for him, but learned,
His tender soul already flies.
That gloomy time passed by,
I wasn't here to say goodbye.

I miss that gentle Jewish fiddler,
There is no soul in my cathedral.

A Halo of Their Fame

My faded star
Returned en vogue,
They raised the bar,
I jumped it as a frog.

They asked my name,
I answered many times,
The halo of their fame
Reflected in my smiles.

Today, the truth gets in,
For some a chilling shower,
Just Paul versus Led Zeppelin,
Who is a faker of the hour?

I told them many times,
"I am the real Zeppelin,
Unleaded, nice n' wise,
Wearing a happy grin."

My greedy lawyer
Met me in the foyer,
She shook my hand,
"Follow me, honey,
We'll sue the band,
They use your name,
Let's get the money,
Leave them the fame."

An olden chicken game,
Big money versus fame,
Two horses face-to-face,
We surely won the race,
I'm rich. I bought a bank,
A jet, a castle and a tank.

Fame is a blinding fever
Round the famous band,
Wealth is a giant cleaver,
I hold it firmly in my hand.

A Half-Naked Dervish

My qualms roam free,
Dead soldiers ascend
Above the battle slope,
A silent, wounded glee
Still's looking for the end,
According to a horoscope.

A raucous cannonade
Like victory's applause
Will run away and fade
Among our horrid foes.

Wars burden gentle souls,
Boots gladly march again,
The war-machine still rolls,
Dreams disappear in vain.

Life seized my past,
I marched barefoot,
To identify my foes, at last,
I can't forgive, God should.

An old half-naked dervish
Stood basking in the sun,
He guessed my final wish,
I didn't want to aim my gun.

Old demons are alive
And will return,
And yet, to live and thrive,
I had more things to learn.

This quiet Bedouin-fakir,
A wise man of the East
Presented me a souvenir,
A secret of celestial feast,
A paradise that gleams,
A grandeur high above,
A harbor for my dreams,
A dome nobody knows of.

A Gritty Path

I'm a hungry seagull,
I'm a white-winged stranger,
I'm a friendless eagle,
I'm a sarcastic fallen angel.

As a rebellious naysayer,
I marched that gritty path,
Nobody heard my prayer,
Numbed by my dire wrath.

Euphoria became a fallen petal,
Life turned into a dry bouquet
Of prematurely wilted roses.
I chose to stay above the fray,
I could no longer hide or settle
Amid hypocrisy of hollow poses.

I'm extricated from common sense,
I'm not a part of boring institutions,
I'm a lonesome disillusioned man,
I often climb over the tallest fence
And seek my own original solutions,
Enjoying every hour of my lifespan.

I sow wholesome seeds of doubt
In every ignorant and lazy head,
Though, even a horrid pain of gout
Will never stop a militant braindead.

The weary trees shed golden leaves,
Cool heads surrender to the dragons,

Hot heads would fight for their beliefs,
Surrounding themselves with wagons.

I failed to make a living as a fighter,
Too many moons passed in a daze,
I pledge to make a living as a writer
In quest of freedom from this maze.

A Greener Grass

I saw a greener grass
Over the broken fence,
I didn't miss my chance,
I came to live in France.

I pen my rhymes in France,
I learn to cook and dance,
I date; I drink a lot of wine,
I bask in the sweet sunshine.

I walk across the pages
Of my unfinished book,
I dare to put my wagers,
Not on a longer fishing line,
But on a self-effacing hook.

Not on another smoggy sign,
But on the court of the divine.

"Dear fisherman
Of human lives,
I am your loyal fan,
Don't let the lies
Affect the truth.
Don't pull my wisdom tooth,
Remove my pains and doubts,
Show your ins and outs,
Attest an eager sinner,
Turn me into a winner."

I took my god sent chance,
I pen my rhymes in France.

A Graveyard of my Tears

I calmly enter my nightmare,
Missing a warning to beware.

I see a giant prison wall
Made of my wasted years,
It is a dungeon for my soul,
A graveyard of my tears.

The pockmarked moon
Mirrors the wounds of war.
My baby, I'll see you soon,
Please don't close the door.

I climb the sizzling slopes,
Totally worn and desolate,
My enemies encircling me,
I send my farewell hopes
Over the desert of my fate
Into the promised glee.

I push into a gaping hole
My restless mind to seethe,
I beg my lifeless soul
To breathe.

I'm seeing an enticing venue:
Your hair of autumn hue,
Your eyes of the ocean blue,
Your flesh I intimately knew,
Your smile's eternal stream,
Pure as a baby's dream…

A Goldfish

I swiftly netted a goldfish,
She sobbed, "I beg you,
Let me go. Just ask,
I'll fulfill your every task,
I'll grant you every wish,
The happy ones or blue."

That fish didn't attempt
To beg me twice,
Nobody wants to tempt
My appetite to rise.

Churchgoers need a pastor,
A carnival entails a barker,
A hero has to have a stunt.
I hardly ever knew a master,
I'm a dog that doesn't hunt,
That doesn't bark and bite.
My shadow is much darker,
If the red lights are bright.

The fish's tendency for lying
Was on a shameful display,
My virginal naiveté is crying,
That fish didn't return to pay.

Months waved, but passed,
The angels blessed my soul,
It's glowing like hot embers,
Scorching my troubled past.
In case, the fish remembers,
I'll exercise my self-control.

A Glitzy Gypsy

A glitzy gypsy,
A dark sidewalk,
I am quite tipsy,
She does the talk.

She reads my lines,
Gods' roads on my palm,
No words, just signs
Of the unknown psalm:
"The wheels will knock,
Your train will run,
The angels will unlock
The room where it has begun".

Somehow she foresaw
An extra power in me
To break the ancient law,
To find the shores of glee,
To learn the sacred word
Which birthed the world.

Much later, in the skies,
I saw the carriers of wombs,
I've heard the mothers' cries,
I touched my buddies' tombs.

Even a dead cat bounced
When lost nine lives and fell,
I entered heaven unannounced
And angels rang the silver bell.

A Future made for Sinners

The pain is always mutual,
The truce is signed, at last,
Each sinner has a future,
Each preacher has a past.

It was a tragic strophe
We coincidentally met,
It's all about do or don't.
Still, it's a catastrophe
When we so sadly get
What we so badly want.

We leaped from barbarism
Into the ditch of decadence,
Ignored a great civilization,
Our world over a rosy prism
Disparages the providence
Of great, but troubled nation.

The ignorance is our key
To lethargy of knowledge,
To stigma of the doomed.
Today, I saw a wartime plea,
The days of bloody carnage
Dropped pants and mooned.

A future made for sinners,
A past is given to the saints,
We pick the smiley winners,
The proof of our wisdom faints.

A Sticky Drop of Fear

My love is a lonely planet,
A ball of wrinkly granite,
Flying above a sea of glee
And asks to be or not to be.

I couldn't run away,
Dark demons came for me,
I couldn't beg or pray,
I froze like a lethargic flea.

They tightly locked the cage,
Sleep well, goodbye, so long.
Sunset didn't erase my rage,
A silent cry went to my song.

A sticky drop of fear
Plowed its way across
The filigree of wrinkles,
It was a lonesome tear,
A stubborn albatross,
A therapy for thinkers.

Love is a lonely planet,
A ball of wrinkly granite.
I lost my chance to flee,
Asking to be or not to be.

The seeds of sour grapes
Destroy our ultimate affairs,
Unstoppable anxiety escapes
Into my traitorous nightmares.

A Star Slid from the Sky

A morning naughty frost
Acts like a friendly host
For fragile sunny beams
Of yet uncertain dreams.

The winters come and go,
The sun may cease a rain,
The brittle flakes of snow
Will melt and never reign.

A few alluring stars still glow
Over the roads endless maze,
The curtains fall after the show
As wilted yesterday's bouquets.

I see a firebird of endless hope
Laughs like a bluebird every dawn,
I know this is not the end of our rope,
I know this is not a singing swan.

A star slid from the sky
To drown in the sea,
I made a wish,
The moon will learn to fly
Across the night of glee.

A Star Has Fallen from the Sky

I ask my angel, "Why do I see
In front of me an empty dish?"
"A star has fallen from the sky,
But you forgot to make a wish".

The candle's crying on my table,
Magician-winter hides the leaves,
It is the final chapter of my fable,
"Amazing grace of naked trees."

It is too late to plow,
It is too late to sow,
The end is here and now,
Before the endless glow.

Heavens are waiting,
I see the sacred glow,
The stars are fading,
It's a good time to go.

A Stairway for a Few

I see the gothic naves
Over the silent waves
Of badly painted night.
The stained-glass lace,
Pierced with the rays
Of the eternal light.

The cold divinity
Of old cathedrals
Filled with infinity
Of baffling riddles.

Enduring dreams
And fragile sounds,
A half-baked dawn
And a sneaky dusk,
Theology of whims
And broken bounds,
Have lost their husk
And bliss has gone.

Just ask the chosen few,
Is there a room for you.

A Spoken Word is Just a Lie

Love makes no sense,
Love lies or chews the fat,
Hate only plays offence,
Hate is an all devouring rat.

As fathers of my fathers'
Father,
As mothers of my mothers'
Mother
During the moody meatless
Times
Of forty agonizing days of
Lent,
We watch the outburst of
Crimes,
But treat it as a nonevent.

I fall in love from time to time
Quietly walking on eggshells,
But love and hate don't rhyme
In my poetic poisoned wells.

I can no longer love and hate,
Both hone my blurry view,
I would prefer to sit and wait
For dazzling morning dew,
For diamonds on the grass,
And wisdom of a crystal glass.

I'm too lethargic for this world.
A spoken or a written word,
In short, it is just a naked lie,
I've gone, farewell, goodbye.

A Poetic Dwarf

Being quite old I gradually morph
Into a dormant bear,
Some critics call me a poetic dwarf,
I let them bark; I hardly even care.

Why are we frugal with ourselves
And yet so generous with others?
Our stanzas lie on dusty shelves,
Nobody reads, nobody bothers.

I entertain my endless guests,
We eat, we drink and all the rest,
I even read to them my rhymes,
But hear the silence of the mimes.

I wander in my winter garden,
The trees are cutely dressed
In sheets of sparkling ice.
My trusting soul was hardened
And I repentantly confessed,
My Lord, I'm tired of your Hell,
Allow me to try your paradise.

A Ploy

Long nights embrace
My rather costly lovers,
My rollercoaster days
Candied my tired face
In sunset's fiery colors.

I praise my voodoo curses,
At night, I carve my verses
Till dawn crawls to my room
As if a witch forgot a broom.

My fate is like a rusty car
With two front blown tires.
When I was young
A cuckoo bird predicted
I'll go high and far.
Then why am I fenced
With barbed wires,
Then why my undertaker
Says hello,
Then why my doctor
Says goodbye,
Then why gods say I owe
Until I reach the sky?

I used to wear my suits
With running down stripes,
Today,
I'm locked up by Uncle Sam,
Jailed with some awful types,

Today,
Each stripe runs crossways
Like a sarcastic epigram.

As whales, I can't forget
The days of splendid joy,
The years of awful pain.
I daily search the internet,
I need a partner for a ploy
To ride a left-the-station train.

A Play

Faith rudely interrupted
My never-ending edgy day
And sharply reconstructed
My own demise into a play.

Faith is a merciless monger,
She sees no foes and friends,
Faith never satisfies her hunger,
Devouring us until the bitter ends,
Until the stars forget to glow,
Until streams cease their flow.

It sounds like a useless adage,
Like a dated, weary aphorism,
Like a futile fruit of knowledge,
Like an old-fashioned cynicism.

A doctor cut my mother's cord,
Before I faced the godsent light,
Before life set my heart on fire,
Before I heard the last accord,
Before the stars turned bright,
I lived a life of Lucifer's desire.

With our picture-perfect gods,
Faith is a clash without fighters,
Men wear their forged façades
Described by famous writers,
Forever known to each one,
But never read by anyone.

A Sin is Not a Crime

A sin is not a crime,
I learned it, just in time.
I heard a cry, "rejoice,
You'll die and hear His voice."

The seven deadly sins
Are peccadilloes,
But without three of them,
Pride, lust and sloth,
My poetry may never
Has been born.
We wouldn't have the unicorn
Identified as being simply Goth.

The answers grow in clay pots,
Bonfires of vanity and greed
Devour dignity and thoughts,
While hell is never guaranteed.

Long life of our poor saints,
Based upon absolute beliefs,
Even my useless preacher faints,
When he detects my bas-reliefs.

The bars of my own prison
Cast shads onto my life,
Cast dimness on the reason,
Behind my ineffective strife.

There is no dull or bright,
There is no black or white

Among the rainbow arches.
Above the military marches,
Thereafter, kneel and kiss
All us who went to the abyss.

A Shipwreck Found

Habitual Parisian bouquinistes
Lined on the banks of the Seine,
Displaying ancient books in tatters.
We stroll like venerable priests,
Mourn losses and flaunt gains,
We know all the liabilities of men,
Today, it's all that really matters,
Dismiss the self-inflicting pains.

Paris-Soir, an evening paper said,
A pirate's shipwreck found,
Time crawls at the snail's pace,
Reluctantly, we move ahead
To hear the trumpet's sound
Raising the drowned to replace.

The news is like a healing balm
Of skillfully veiled crudeness,
It acts as a sacramental psalm,
Critical of vanity and lewdness.

With our black-eyed minds,
With fearful and misty wills,
Like horses with the blinds,
We gallop to the smoky hills
As rarely agitated go-getters
To catch our hiding debtors.

Time flies, greed only crawls,
Both merchandise our souls.

A Beacon

Our prophets learned
There is no happy life,
Our paradise is earned
After a never-ending strife.

We mimic brainless fools,
We waste our shiny ways,
We follow reckless rules,
We fade and leave no trace.

We cherish our happy days,
The rest invisibly pass by,
We gather bits of happiness
To build a beacon in the sky.

We'll arrive to wisdom,
It won't be hard to prove,
There is no happy kingdom,
Only a shallow groove.

The leaves will thrive
On naked trees of death,
The bliss of endless life
Will hear our final breath.

A Rose Without Thorns

I hold a tender flower,
A rose without thorns,
Meanwhile a sunlit shower
Compassionately mourns.

Her virgin years
Come to the end,
She wipes her tears.
No wedding band.

A mighty fever
Struck her heart
And eager flesh.
She is so fresh.
I'm showing her
That love is art.

She's a gorgeous guest,
She is so beautifully kind,
I try to be a gracious host
We're both on our quest,
In vain, we try to find
What we have never lost.

Those years have gone,
I hardly find any time
To search for someone.
I'm silent as a swan,
I'm beyond my prime,
I'm a voiceless mime.

Only a fluctuating logic
Still entertains my mind,
Flames of eternal magic
Leave darkness far behind.

I fill my famished pages
With melancholic strophes,
I plan to live through ages
And earn poetic trophies.

A Saint Must Have A Past

A saint must have a past,
A sinner needs tomorrows,
Soul is a broken plaster cast,
A mausoleum hiding sorrows.

I hear the midnight tunes
Of lonesome nightingales,
While quiet silver moons
Guard secrets of my tales.

The memories are often fruitless,
They bring the scars of our flares,
They never bring back goodness
And joy of our passionate affairs.

My scarred and wrinkled face
Etched on a coffin of my years,
I miss the one I would embrace,
She was a witness of my fears.

She left; the skies had flipped,
She left; bliss fell in the abyss,
The angry branches whipped
The bodies of uprooted trees.

My mind is a quaint enclave,
It is a boneyard of my whims,
But I'm still alive and crave
The advent of my dreams.

A Seraphim-Avenger

I'm guilty in the verdict of a court,
I'm only innocent before my angel,
I lost, they tossed me overboard,
I'll become a seraphim-avenger.

My hyperbolic language,
My apocalyptic prophecy,
May seem a disadvantage
In my perpetual odyssey.

No one can take
A correspondence course
Of incarceration and hard labor.
No one can fake
A genuine remorse
Of one who hates his neighbor.

The ends won't justify the means,
Reruns are draped in sunny rays,
Perplexing psychedelic dreams
Bring onward their eccentric days.

I crave to welcome anxious truth
Locked in a prison with my youth.

I'm a machete-wielding poet,
I fight between my rhymes,
I'm frank; I let you know it,
I didn't commit those crimes.

My boat is safer in the harbor,
It's probing for a place to hide
Behind compassion of the law.
I pace under the rainbow-arbor,
My conscience fights my mind,
If someone wins, I sign the draw.

A Shattered Lineage

A shattered lineage
Of my written thoughts
Looks like a mirrored image
Of slowly sinking riverboats.

I often write about scars
Left by the orbits of the dice
Behind the rusty prison bars
Round the birds of paradise.

I'm in pursuit of my reality,
Striking the iron while it's hot,
I have no time to cross the t,
I have no I to place the dot.

My horses left the barn,
My train has left the station,
I substitute goddamn by darn,
But can't abolish my frustration.

I never know where I go,
I rarely know where I am,
I never see the clouds flow,
Unless I'm in a traffic jam.

Time doesn't flow anymore,
My brothers fight a futile war,
Young starlets climb the ladder,
The amateurs still run the show,
And even Jesus at the Seder
Said to those twelve, "I know."

A Sheep That Lost Her Ram

Our infidelities
Don't rip our families,
It happens only
When we get caught,
Then we become so lonely,
We'd sail a sinking boat.

It's late; I try to hit the sack,
I see her through a window,
She is wearing only black,
Is she a mourning widow?

Is she
A sheep that lost her ram?
Is she
As sad and lonely as I am?

Life is a vacant throne,
A needle with no thread,
A nightmare falls alone
Into my icy, empty bed.

My good old friends
Are dead or far away,
Some other hands
Caressing me today.

I outlived my time,
Desire to be has gone,
I'm a lonesome mime,
I'd still enjoy someone.

These days, I'm not alone,
I have a loyal chaperone,
She is
A sheep that lost her ram,
She is
As sad and lonely as I am.

A River of Nightmares

A stream of bitter salty tears
Runs under the wisdom tree,
A river of nightmares and fears
Runs into the eager thirsty sea.

I'm rolling in my crumpled bed
Like a bitch begging for a treat,
As if the lights are always red
On her deserted lifelong street.

There is no one to kiss and hold,
I gambled with my love and lost,
I didn't learn how to lose or fold,
Today, I learned she won't return
At any cost.

I've seized momentum,
Enough of bitter losses,
The angel fell. I won't lament him,
I fly above the stars and crosses.

A Fountain Without Water

My peerless fight
Held a muted sadness,
It stopped at night
Within a void of madness.

I didn't flip the silver quarter,
But I was numb and strange,
I was a fountain without water,
I was a bendy, leafless branch.

I was married to a grump
Through thick and thin,
I never played a trump,
I had no chance to win.

My wings did not unfurl,
I was perpetually wrong,
I never finished first,
I never caught that bird,
I never kissed that girl,
I never sang that song,
Too poorly versed,
I was a weary nerd.

I only loved my loyal dog,
From beginning to the end,
A humble hero of my epilogue,
My sweetheart, bosom friend.

Dawn brought a baby day
Wrapped up in laughter,
My dog and I found our way
To happiness forever after.

A Sequel

I climbed the rainbow arc
To see its magic bend,
I plunged into the dark,
My life foretold its end.

While the stardust settles,
There are no stables for a day,
No horses, reins and saddles,
I stroll along the Milky Way.

A day without fear,
A day without strife
Is brighter than a year
Of empty, fruitless life.

My body and my soul
Totally separate but equal,
Both dancing on the pole
In premonition of a sequel.

A Fool no More

The bubbles burst,
I stomp across the puddle.
Am I the last, am I the first
Among the human rubble?

I have no use for preachers,
I'm a sinner to my core,
I'm too old
For these lethargic teachers,
I'm a fool no more.

I hate those so-called
Moral guards
And their devoted friends.
To them we're just houses
Of cards,
The sadists have no merci,
No amends.

Lackluster roads of goodbyes
Stream to the world unknown,
Without our good and evil,
Without our sins and virtues,
Without our dissolutions.
Yet our sun will also rise
Above the same old tortures,
Above the same tombstones,
Above the same,
But resting in peace illusion

A Fistful of Days

Only a fistful of days
Spanned while in our bus,
The gray highways
Brought down all of us.

Life lost its vibrant colors
It's back to black and white
Inside a golden frame.
It's not a pretty sight,
Old books, new scholars,
New songs, yet old refrain.

Only the blind and senseless
Reject life's change,
Those who don't see, don't
Care,
My life is a shooting range,
A loud, violent and swanky
Love affair.

I'm confused, I'm looking up,
"God, give me a few years,
Don't yet give me that cup,
Forgive my rights and wrongs.
I promise,
You'll never see my tears.
Just let me write my songs
And you'll hear my laughter.
I beg; I kneel before the altar."

A Fiddler on the Roof

The violins can cry,
But only when we sigh,
The violins can laugh,
But only when we love.

There's a fiddler on the roof,
An icon of a great Chagall,
Sincerely heartfelt yet aloof,
Tearing the cloud as a gull.

I hear the deepest sadness
In his heartbreaking tune,
I hear a melody of madness
Soars to the silver moon.

His music breaks old bounds,
The moon swims in the lake,
The ripples rock the sounds
Of crying in the Jewish wake.

The fiddler wraps in pleasures
Our calm before the storm,
Our forever-relished treasures,
Our exceptions from the norm.

A Few Truisms

The words are sharper,
The images are crisper,
Ideas are much brighter
Delivered by a whisper.

In times, our bodies bend,
At times, they even break,
A foe becomes a friend
Or melts like a snowflake.

We learn much more
Than meets the eye,
If we're born to crawl,
We'll never learn to fly.

We use for yodeling songs
Our southern twang and drawl,
We rarely argue or debate
To know rights from wrongs,
We simply instigate
A barroom brawl.

Laziness is ancient art
Of resting in advance,
Only a go-getting heart
Gives work a chance.

When good embraces evil
Most pastors lose their jobs,
Their lies begin to shrivel,
Our silence turns to sobs.

Religion with its angels
Was organized for all
To camouflage avengers.
They fly, the angels fall.

We're religious enough
To hate, but not to love.

A Faithful Custodian

I walked a shaky podium
And read my poetry to you,
I was a faithful custodian
Of matters always tangible,
Yet, sometimes changeable,
But candid as a morning dew.

I wrote about war and peace,
I wrote about nights and days,
I wrote about loves and hates,
I never wrote a masterpiece,
I never wrote a single phrase
That linked me with the greats.

I fed Elijah; I'm one of the ravens,
I celebrate my excommunication,
I chose to live below the heavens,
Agnostics thrilled me with ovation.
I'm free to worship the Big Bang
Or fly my circles as a boomerang.

There's a silver lining
Baked in every cake,
There's no pointless whining,
There's no apology to make,
In wars, I won each battle,
Why do the sabers rattle?

I hope my lines won't die in vain,
In wars, there are no unwounded,
Even the fallen wounded

Those who are left behind,
The scars were deemed insane
And drained into a silent peace.
Utopian thoughts were ill defined.
While we cooked black-eyed peas,
The pessimists already guessed
Our warmongers will be blessed.

Below Lighthouses of Hopes

I beg you, flying cranes,
Unfurl your mighty wings,
Above the passing years,
Above the passing trains,
Above the passing springs,
Above the farewell tears.

Below lighthouses of hopes,
Below the seas of dreams,
I'm a fighter on the ropes,
Life's harder than it seems.

A devilishly tough debate,
Or just a vapid conversation?
I always choose, in any rate,
The former destination.

Precarious veering rides
Quietly lured me to the cliff,
Death's waiting for my error,
I fall into the hungry tides,
The sea is numb with grief,
I rest beneath a daily terror.

Beheading Poets

I locked my laurels in a cage,
Trying to lull my anger.
The sea has yet another fish,
My life has yet another page,
Which I'll turn and wish
It won't become my strangler.

I'm not out of the woods,
I slide into a muddy pit,
Yet hope to soar one day.
My critics wear their hoods
And gather all their wit
To never let me fly my way.

Their wishes to destroy
Are valuable, creative urges,
Their hardhearted, fatal ploy
Helps to eliminate the purges.

It takes awhile
Before they move ahead
With what has to be done.
Even their being is too vile
For those self-flagellations
In front of guillotines,
Beheading our great poets
Before their coronations.

Behold the Man

Two days after the Supper
We draped Him in a shroud,
Death has arrived to crucify,
Nobody dared to stop her
Among the wicked crowd,
Although, some tried to cry.

I was just one of two,
Who had no name,
I was just one of two
Who had no fame,
I was a thief, the third,
I wept, nobody heard.

When Pontius pronounced
"Behold the man!"
I didn't whimper even once,
Nor now, nether then.

The Calvary procession,
A shame of our passion.
Golgotha was the place,
They said, I was a thief,
No one yet knew my face,
Nobody sighed in grief.

I also dragged the cross,
They didn't pierce my side,
They kindly broke my leg,
I'm a lonesome albatross,

I'm alive, the others died,
That night, I wouldn't beg.

Old Josef brought the shroud,
White as the weightless cloud,
We witnessed His descend
Into the depth of bloody Hell,
We witnessed His ascend,
He raised, I wished Him well.

After the Judas' kiss
He went to live in bliss,
I chose the hellish Earth,
I took the upper berth.

Before the Grill or Glory

Life is a fable for my verse,
Life is a constant intercourse
Of food and wine,
Of love and hate,
Life is a blusterous sunshine,
Life is a godsend dreary fate.
Life is a perversity
Of common views,
Life is a diversity
Of loves we choose.

I hear the weeping birds
And whisper of the trees,
The elegies without words
And drums of war and peace.
Life is a purgatory
Before the grill or glory.

It has been said,
Without a god
A man is dead,
A man is trash,
He's good-for-nothing,
He's just a lifeless thing.
Bliss is a faked façade,
Faith is a smoking ash.

I outlived my gods. Goodbye.
Under the stars earthbound,
My conscience sleeps alone,
No truths or lies around,

No friends or foes nearby
To blame or to condone.

My days are numbered,
Remaining nights are few,
Even my soul is plundered
By crafty pastors of my pew.
December of my life,
A time to buy a cask,
A time to write the will
For a few trophies of my strife.
A time to wear a happy mask
Before I face the devil's grill.

Before the Final Countdown

New fashion thrives in Paris-town,
Strange types pace up and down,
It's my generation of "has-beens",
We still wear torn-apart blue jeans.

I spill the wine of autumn gloom,
I pay the fine for honoring a tomb
With a half-erased and wilted sign,
"Here's resting Gertrude Stein,"
And something else in French.
I curse while drinking on the bench.

I think while looking at the graves
That one who kills is one who saves.

The soulless pitted olives,
Like shingles in the brine,
Remind me of new lowlifes,
Improving their bloodline.

These days, I cross the t's,
I's don't require any dots.
They descend from bliss
As disappointed blood clots.

Tailwinds and obstacles
Don't ever matter,
I pick from paper articles
The former and the latter,
But if I ask for liberty,
Life gives me death

And walks me to infinity
To catch my breath.

I will be buried in Pere Lachaise,
The famous cemetery of Paris-town,
Where every tomb is a showcase
Of hopes before the final countdown.

Before the Flower Froze

I watch the parting play
Of falling golden leaves,
The winter's white ballet
Of swirling snowflakes.
Somebody always gives,
Somebody always takes.

Today, she is eighteen,
She is a blooming rose,
She doesn't want to wait,
She craves the primal sin.
Before the flower froze,
I reap the sweetest bait.

The boats still rock,
The winds still roar,
The gulls still flock,
The sails still soar.

The leaden clouds
Tightly seal the sky,
The sun rules far above
The unpredicted crowds.
We're in a selfless love,
We've yet to say goodbye.

Before My Imminent Arrest

Before my imminent arrest
I'm the one who knows best,
I have no sign of any valor,
Just a pretentious glamour
And shrouded self-interest,
Over the sullied goodness
With fripperies of lewdness.

My poetry still strolls,
It doesn't have to rush,
It may continue forever,
The magic of black holes
May pull a royal flush,
Whatever and whenever.
The horsemen will appear
And say, "the end is near."

I often think about death,
She comes and leaves
The void of nonexistence
Without innocence of breath,
Without crooks and thieves,
Without a futile coexistence.

Believers call it a Glory train,
To me it is a never-ending pain,
To me it is a sad meat-wagon,
Feeding the fire-breathing dragon.

Barcelona

Inhaling fumes of mango,
Alluring like a love affair,
We danced a torrid tango
Across a Catalonian flare.

My worries came and went,
I was inspired by her glow,
Enchanted by her scent.
The tango kept its flow.

I was a tourist in wonderland,
I kissed her trembling hand,
She let me play the game,
I am sure she knew my aim.

She had a tender grace
Of a devoted gentle swan,
Our footsteps drew a lace
Lit by the sleepless dawn.

I love that most amazing night,
I love you, sparkly Barcelona;
Two loving angels in the flight,
But each no longer is a loner.

I held her strapless shoulders,
The tango fused us into one.
We knew as truthful beholders,
Our farewell has quietly begun.

Banalities Aside

Life isn't fated,
Banalities aside,
Let's go to the core.
Don't try to hide
Behind the dated
Less is more.

At times, it's just a flirt,
I'm the one to blame,
My heart is on alert,
Life is a bloody game.

The battlefield of love,
Isn't a theatre for a dove,
You win, enjoy the thrill,
You lose, get on the grill.

In every real game
One wins, not both,
I'd rather be a flame,
I'd hate to be a moth.

A Prized Utopian Dream

I'm nervous, bite my nails,
Love isn't flat and straight
Like shiny polished rails
Acquainted with my fate.

Our journey living in a mirror,
In pictures of an endless joy,
Chopped by a brutal cleaver
Into the ruins of a cruel ploy.

We live as captives of a siege,
While our aimless ship of fools
Passing under a drawbridge
With laziness of rented mules.

Don't let our feelings chill,
Don't hurt our love, don't kill,
When someone walks away,
Hearts break, it's not a play.

We're rambling with our doubts,
Descending to a sensual abyss,
Life is arranging ruthless bouts
Between fine hell and foul bliss.

Love is a prized utopian dream,
Love is a quickly moving stream,
It's fading from the scene of crime,
Forever, but in silence of a mime.

Infinity Without Dawn

The chimneys puff,
The stars are bright,
The moon makes love
To secrets of the night.

My life was spent
As gleaming solitaire
Trying to unleash itself
Within a naughty crowd.
The tragic truth is bent,
While *Candid* by Voltaire
Chained to a dusty shelf
Uselessly vain and proud.

The cotton balls of clouds
Sail over the endless skies,
Wrapped in the shrouds
Before my tickled eyes.
Each one of them was born
As so-called normal people;
After the cords were torn,
They climb the steeple.

Then everybody dies
Just as a chosen one
And wins the prize--
Infinity without dawn.

An Incurable Disease

I hung
Her photo on the wall,
I swung
My head toward the hall,
She stood like a mirage,
By herself, no entourage,
I try to rescue this shipwreck,
"I'm sorry, take me back."

I grew to be a master,
Attentive, kind and brave,
But she saw a disaster,
No one would ever crave.

I love; I fight and play,
The pendulums still sway,
Age is an incurable disease,
No one can stop or cease.
.

I've seen this film before,
It's daily tit-for-tat,
And rainy days keep score.
Take my unsolicited advice,
No one can enter
The same river twice.

I'm Lost…

I'm lost in the labyrinths of sadness,
Between the twigs of time long past.
The grandeur of the sunset's redness
Leads into the promised glee at last.
The never-ending gloom
Reminds me of the sea,
While stormy clouds loom,
And seagulls fly carefree.
I wander in an open field,
I try to hug you in the haze,
But muddled years of guilt
Conceal your gorgeous face.
You're a morning after,
You're a forbidden fruit,
You're a tune of laughter
Played on a magic flute.
My precious life, I love you,
You're my endless feast,
You're my morning dew,
You're my sunlit East.

There is no void
Between my lines,
Don't get annoyed,
Just read the warning signs.

Axiomatic Truths

Desire to learn is our treasure,
A decent teacher's worth the fee,
The bottom line is our pleasure,
We learn; we are forever free.

The roots of trees are often bitter,
Only the fruits are sweet,
These verses aren't for a quitter,
But for the one I'd like to meet.

I have not seen bad students,
Just many mediocre teachers,
Their lack of poise and prudence
Creates our cunning preachers.

Our tomorrows need two features,
My aphorisms don't need your bids,
Don't hire these moronic teachers,
Remember, they'll teach OUR kids.

Away the Clouds Flew

Life is a round trip,
My better foot
Steps forward
Into the fairytale.
I didn't jump my ship,
I didn't drop my loot,
Just mark my word,
I wasn't born to fail.

Away the clouds flew
Along the doubts flow,
Above the chosen few
Whose vivid halos glow.

How are you, Madam Day?
How are you, Mister Night?
I march the same old way,
I have to breathe and fight.

My God, I've had enough,
Please, let your servant go,
Unlock my golden cage.
A teardrop of your love,
A morning puff you blow,
Should turn a better page.

Don't lead me to the gate,
It's still too early for my life,
It's a conclusion of my fate,
To start again and thrive.

I'll breathe this chance
I'll find the time to pray,
I thank you in advance
For giving me the day.

Au Revoir, Mon Ami

I wrote a debatable treatise
About my resurgent loves
Of youthfully clever pretties,
About gentle, loving doves
Involved in tough debates
About our lives and fates,
Moving their baffled days
Along Parisian walkways.

The golden leaves are busy
Whispering while falling down.
It's autumn. The rain's freezing
Across majestic Paris-town.

Goodbye, our endless nights,
Au revoir, my witty friend,
So long, my Mecca of delights,
Please, tell me, is this the end?

Never to stroll along La Rue Ravioli,
Never to see La Place de la Concorde
Never to cross Le Jardin de Tuileries
Will Paris cut its mother's cord?
Will the sky cry with morning dew?
I hear, Le Blues du Bebe Heureux.

I won't return
To hug and kiss you, mon ami,
I promise, I'll learn
To cherish memories of glee.

At Night All Cats Seem Gray

The rain-loaded clouds
Cry over autumn's gold,
Throw away your doubts,
This winter has to fold.

The hounds and retrievers,
The mermaids of the rivers,
Let's start our hunting game,
Collect yourselves and aim.

I sing my lullabies to crimes,
Committed in the daily maze,
I write my gloomy rhymes
As a sad diary of tragic days.

Wherever the grass is greener,
Call me; I'm a naughty boy,
Call me; I'm a careless sinner,
Call me; I'm a worshiper of joy.

You come to me at night
To play,
To talk and love by candlelight,
Where no one is a predator
Or prey,
Nobody has an urge to fight,
At night, all cats seem gray.

At Last

The dissonance in our lives
Grants harmony to our lies.

Tomorrow's guilty pleasure
Morphs our daily garbage
Into a nasty neighbor-geezer
Who seeks a forged salvation.
He is a saber-rattling savage
That vends a cruel treasure,
Of the masochistic squeezer
Who likes the pain's duration.

He knows in advance
A failure from success,
He also combs the miles
Of our disappointing lives.

At last, we rest in peace,
Don't lament, please...

Ascension

The loud vicious ravens fly
In premonition of a gory war,
Some drown in champagne
And caviar,
Some are in pain but never
Cry,
The evil spirits and the saints
Keep score,
They always know who we are.

I am afraid that our freedom
Is closer than a generation
From extinction.
I live and hope to find a cure
For this dreadful affliction.

I am suspicious of farewells,
I am suspicious of goodbyes,
I disregard these parallels,
I only trust my mother's eyes.

The shock of earlier distress
Handcuffed my will to live,
Bliss has the same address
As our Lord who may forgive.

My path to hell was paved
Without my attention,
The devil and the saints
Learned how I behaved,
And didn't cast their votes
For my ascension.

Ascending to the Throne

A tangled bottom fell,
I wrote my final song
About bliss and hell,
About right and wrong.

I ran my solo marathon,
Ascending to the throne.

I left behind my luggage,
Brushed it aside at last,
I dumped the roughage
Of my dilapidated past.

I sailed the lakes at dusk
I sailed the seas at dawn,
It was forbidden to a duck,
But was allowed to a swan.

I saw my humble savior
Beyond the finish line,
He was my guiding carrier,
A messenger of all divine.

I ran my solo marathon,
But didn't reach the throne.

Art is a Drunkard

Law and order reassure,
While power and money lure,
Art is a drunkard at the curb,
The arts get sober to disturb.

Art bursts the loudspeakers,
As someone cries or sings,
Frustrated pleasure seekers,
We're just boxing in the rings.

I want a constant dawn,
I want a spotless love,
I want my troubles gone,
I think I've had enough.

I crawl across the thinnest ice,
I won't ever pray or preach,
But I'm on the way to paradise.
Regrettably, it's out of my reach.

I clinch my fists and fight,
I slash my wrists at night.
I'm just a chinwag whore,
I have no better metaphor.

Arrows into The Well

Rain falls on planet Earth
Over the sins of wilted flowers,
Like all celebrities at birth
The saints enjoy cold showers.

Rain plays its strings,
Above the hungry grounds,
I hear the tunes of springs
And waterfalls of sounds.

Even the wholesome rains
Innocently pour for hours,
And wash away the pains
From nearly lifeless flowers.

The scorching sun is bright
Over the thirsty olive trees
Of Gethsemane.
Coincidences don't exist;
The trees cheer in the rain.
In solidarity: I raise my fist
Toward the beams of light,
Toward the gods of peace.

It's not the never-ending rain
Threw arrows into the well,
It's my soul's agonizing pain
Sent my teardrops of farewell.

Argonauts

A siren's gentle song
Pierces the dormant sky,
The tired sailors sweetly sleep,
The nights are hardly ever long;
Their nightly silence knows why
The clouds sorrowfully weep.

Our journey lasted twenty years,
Like Homer's fearless Argonauts
On a quest for the Golden Fleece.
Our wives, amid the other thrills
Guessed loves and loves me nots.
A young Odysseus's Penelope
Maintained her precious hope.

A manna from heaven
Delivers us from Hell,
Among the deadly seven,
We find a place to dwell.
Our mental constipation,
Our sacred safety feature,
Creates a congregation
Much wiser than its preacher.
Our sinless mothers
Cut the cord
And pray for progress
In the world.

Intelligence won't learn to die,
The fools won't learn to fly
Above exciting movie plots.

We march as proud Argonauts,
We fight to win; we cross the line,
But cast the pearls for any swine.

Our curiosity won't fly;
Our science is asleep.
I'm Jason, I know why
Our tomorrows weep.

Archnemeses

Two great archnemeses at large,
Always together, Good and Evil
Ask me to guess who's in charge
And who'll fall under the cleaver.

A dusty window to my soul
Shows St. Peter and St. Paul,
Who never let me see inside,
To meet my vanity and pride.

Today, nobody won, nobody lost,
At times, a draw is a better end.
A sluggish flow past the riverbend,
It's Rubicon that wasn't crossed
To trace the rays of God sent lights,
Instead, we guard the starry nights.

Even the longest twine
Comes to the end,
The moon is gone,
Rung by the stars,
The night falls silent,
Slain by a puny dawn.
It's time to dot the i's,
It's time to cross the t's,
It's time to see the line,
It's time to rest in peace.

Arabesque

My eager heart is like a hungry shark,
Although its destiny rests in my hand.
A "Vacant" sign is glowing in the dark,
These rooms are for a one-night stand.

A dusty shelter for the morbid prowler,
A road motel with moldy rooms inside;
The owners named it "Eiffel Tower",
An accolade to our vanity and pride;
A sad reminder of our long embrace,
It is the outstanding pinnacle of grace,
That soars over our undisputed might.
My tender heart is like a fading spark,
Gentle and calm like an Easter flower,
When I am in love, it glows in the dark
And flies above the real Eiffel Tower.

I took the bait,
The night in that motel
Was truly great,
But I don't kiss and tell.

Anxiety

I camouflaged eternal faintness
And soared into the vanities' abyss;
I reached an earthly greatness
And vanished into the virtues' bliss.

The paradigms of self-esteems
Like cemeteries for the dreams
Survived anxiety from critics' raids
Under the quilts of darker shades.

It was not a picture-perfect time
To be an artist-hero,
And yet, I had to pay a pretty dime
For Andy Warhol's case of "Brillo".
For Mark Rothko's illusory stress
And for Jackson Pollok's mess.

That moment, everything went wrong,
The monolith of my illusions fell apart,
But just a single song
Survived the vicious art
Of unimaginable anxiety of death,
Of life beyond the parting breath.

I am not a vigorous defender
Of our constant dissonance of rules;
Even the cows change their gender
When hear the tramping raging bulls.

We frame and hang our tinted souls,
We illustrate the Dead Sea scrolls,
We engineer our ostentatious arts,
But never mend our bleeding hearts.

Another Youth is Stolen

The battles come and go,
The war meat grinders stay,
A piercing, saber-rattling flow
Invites cannon fodder to play.

Unknown youth,
Unknown graves
And silent crosses
Face my windows.
Only the bitter truth
About our braves,
Carries for widows
Their bloody losses.

I drink a sour, vinegary wine,
At the burial of a friend of mine,
I'm drunk, I walk across
Abandoned diamonds of dew.
And yet I'm a daring albatross
That landed from the blue,
To stomp a silent battlefield,
A mausoleum of the killed.

A cacophony of rhetoric
Wakes the not-yet-fallen.
In every trigger's click
Another youth is stolen.

Another Song has Died

Another song has died,
I wrote its dreary beat,
I try to have another ride
And take the empty seat.

I see the looming sun
Above a morning haze,
Another winter's gone
Without any love or praise.

So long, cold winter's breath,
So long, cold winter's life,
So long, cold winter's death,
I'm just trying to survive.

The lanterns sway,
The birds don't sing,
Rainfall is on its way.
Good morning, spring.

The rite of spring,
Young girls love in their sleep,
But wake to see a melted snow.
A red snowbird begins to sing,
And fights the mirror of my Jeep
And never lets it go.

Another Hot July

Another hot July,
The sun won't pass,
The birds forget to fly,
A raven clears her throat,
A rabbit nibbles
On the juicy grass
And sweats into his hairy coat.
Meanwhile, I write my scribbles.

All of a sudden, like a train,
Rain rushes to the ground,
I'm quite wonderfully insane
And imitate this dusty sound.

I'm unruly, I'm quite rogue,
I cry like melting ice,
I have a grave to dig
For my new verse.
I fail to see a log
In my own eyes,
But see a tiny twig
In yours.

I press my rhymes
Through the tightest sieves,
I hear the swaying chimes,
I hear the swirling leaves,
I hear the drops of rain,
I wish never to write in vain,
I hope someone forgives,
That I may dream sometimes.

Under the nightly flow,
The less I know,
The better is my sleep,
Just never ask me why I weep.

Another Gray-Haired Winter

Another gray-haired winter,
My mom moans at the door,
The snow falls upon her lintel,
Her son fights somebody's war.

I'm alive, the bullets missed,
I only heard the whistles,
I'm christened by the beast,
By horrid glowing missiles.

I'm back, the end of quest,
First hug in many years,
Few medals on my chest,
My mom sheds happy tears.

Boys are forever boys,
We're no heroes 'til we died,
We earned these medals-toys,
Meanwhile our mothers cried.

My mom still worries from the sky,
I hocked my uniform and medals,
So many gloomy moons passed by,
Time stopped, I pushed the pedals,
Shrewd politicians moved their lips,
These useless cowards always lied,
While they were taking leisure trips,
My dearest brothers fought and died.

Boys fought as boys,
They earned their toys.

Another Fable

Red leaves and rainy beads
Swirl in the nervous skies,
Another autumn bleeds,
Another autumn cries...

Late autumn drops its leaves,
They fondly fall into my palms;
I only feel my pains and griefs,
I only hear the wartime bombs.

They stole my careless years,
They stole my brightest days,
My silent laughs and tears,
My nights and sunny rays.

Even if the sky still glistens,
I have no time for cheers,
Caught in the spider lace;
I know God just listens,
But sadly, never hears;
Only the fallen angel saves.

Even the longest rope,
Sooner-or-later has to end;
It's time to judge the thieves,
Life gave us time and hope,
Let's burn the autumn leaves,
And every sinner will ascend.

Annie

She walked across the street,
So graceful, tall and slender,
A composed energy of truth,
A gorgeous swan-like caravel
Flaunting a blinding splendor
Of its unblemished youth.

Love pushed the break,
And everybody swiftly stopped:
Champagne, a wedding cake,
A dance; the curtains dropped.

Her name was Annie,
Her gentle, elongated face
Reminded me of Modigliani.

Sweet cupids sent their darts,
We passionately fell in love
Then married, never parted,
Drowning in sex and arts,
We never had enough,
And felt as if we only started.

Three passionate, elated years
Unnoticeably passed by;

Poor Annie died;
Swept by a river of my tears.
I didn't have to say goodbye,
We're still floating alongside.

And Yet

Love goddess is born in the sea,
And married to a god of fire,
We sail once becoming free
Into the slavery of our desire,
Our lives are brought from glee
Into the flames of the aroused ire.

The tunes of trumpets flow
Above our disappointed pride,
The words are cruelly thrown,
The cozy feelings piled aside,
And yet, love is unknown
To those who never cried,
And yet, the end is known
Only to those who died.

Touching Sacred Grounds

I am between tomorrow
and today,
I am between the skies
and Earth,
I am between the doves
and birds of prey,
I am between demise and birth.

I am a hungry red-tailed falcon,
I am a crafty ash-leafed sage,
I still bring home the bacon
As our elders used to say.
Soon, I will read my final page,
But hope to see another day.

I know alliance from disdain,
I am bored, I am almost gone,
I can no longer bear the pain,
And yet, long live new dawn!

I combed dustbins of yesteryears,
I counted our wins and losses;
There were no wins without tears,
There were no losses
Without David's stars or crosses,
Without weeping willows
Bending to the graves
And touching sacred grounds,
Where our fallen heroes
Rest in peace on rocky pillows.

Wars kill. I hope God saves
For a few extra rounds.

I didn't talk myself into the gloom,
I laid fresh roses on another tomb;
My heroes couldn't beat the odds,
I wouldn't whistle past graveyards.

A Vault of Hope

I watch a morbid march
Of self-inflicting doubts,
Under the crispy starch
Of aimless cotton clouds.

Nostalgic dreams at work,
Most problems of today
Morph into the morrows,
We're waiting for a stork,
Good flies above the fray,
Evil remains in burrows.

The great Messiah came,
Then went to join his Dad,
I wonder, whom to blame
A good, an ugly or a bad?
All three stand on my way,
All three brought lovely gifts,
Three wise men of today,
Under the star that drifts.

I'm clever as an owl,
But I am yet not blind
And see another war.
It's not a proper day
To lose my mind
And throw a towel,
Then shut the door
And fly above the fray.

The rockets and warplanes
Cast shadows on the slope,
Soaked with the bullet's rains,
And yet, I see a vault of hope.

It is a dialectic flare
In the eternal freeze,
I sense a love affair
Of war and peace.

A Triangle of Madness

We finished our song
With a dramatic end,
In vain, we sadly longed
For our angel to descend.

My square of sadness
Eagerly grasped for air,
Her triangle of madness
Shrieked on the phone,
"It is the end of our affair,
You'll learn to live alone."

I see over a bluff
Red birds of hate,
Blue birds of love
Flew in too late.

Hope's dying in the grass
Under the bleeding skies,
Love is a shattered glass,
A great illusion in disguise.

Another broken plea,
Another love is dead,
The red sunset of glee,
It's so insufferably sad.

A Tragic Harlequin of Joy

Life fell into my hands,
As never-ending rails,
As everlasting heavens.
A rainbow elegantly bends,
I listen to the nightingales,
But hear the feisty ravens.

Lights drown in the sea,
The end of a daily bread,
Time heals the pain of glee,
But can't wake up the dead.

Life's going on,
I'm awake; it's dawn,
I put too many irons
In the devouring fire,
I hear the singing sirens,
Elusive objects of desire.

I stroll across a foggy field,
I'm a tragic harlequin of joy,
My sacred envelope is sealed,
I'm a captive of the devil's ploy.

I comb through murky days
Along ambivalence of doubts,
He locked me in the maze
Without ins and outs

A Tragedy to Those Who Feel

A comedy to those who think,
A tragedy to those who feel,
I have to balance on the brink
Of the eternal real and unreal.

Gods hear my cries and laughs,
From two ancient masks of arts,
I live between two equal halves,
Between the minds and hearts.

I have to choose
From comedy and drama,
Bare feet or shoes,
From alpha to omega,
I run along both halves
From health to trauma,
I fly amidst my laughs
From Earth to Vega.

Life is a room inside four walls,
Tears, laughter, love and hate,
The tightly woven quilt of souls
Is just a cozy blanket of my fate.

A Total Silence

Dusks of dementia galore,
I'm reaping what life's sown,
Today and yesterday no more,
I'm forgetting what I've known.

Somebody sold my house
And moved me to a bunker.
Who's that pessimistic louse?
Who's that half-baked hunker?

Satan discovered a weaker link
In my not up to snuff defense,
I didn't have a stretch to blink,
Before I lost my common sense.

The golden fall lies on the ground,
I see a spooky skeleton of winter,
A total silence, nowhere bound,
I'm a mad and lonely sprinter
Running between the shady lines,
Ignoring unfamiliar warning signs.

Bystanders skidded to a halt,
They saw the advent in the making,
To them I was a hill above a vault,
Amid the swirls of a decisive faking,
Bewitchingly magnetic and obscure.
I realized, for us there is no cure.

A Thrown Dice

Life is a great surprise.
Why shouldn't death be
An even greater one?
When our days capsize,
We meet the Holy Three
Or none.

My weary memory delivers
A few buddies from the past,
Their faces flow like the rivers,
Like water that already passed.
My loneliness cannot reenter
The same old water twice.
Life doesn't return a thrown dice.

Another year passed like a dart,
Ignored my body, took my heart.

I'm not scared of the hereafter,
I'll find a solace in every case,
When you'll hear my laughter,
Remember me. I won the race.

A Subtle Harmony

I brought a subtle harmony
To our apprehensive hearts,
Old-fashioned sweetness
Of my sardonic, spicy irony
Spun souls toward the arts
And bodies to completeness.

I redefined those troubles
That relaxing on my mind,
I busted virtue of the bubbles
Of that ancestral, dated bind.

Winged angels think I'm dead,
Saints know I'm a fallen tree,
I'm charged for a daily bread,
Although, I used to get it free.

I play the strings of beams,
Soft clouds flank the skies,
My restless past still dreams,
My tranquil future sadly cries.

I went to pick my mail,
It was a cheery envelope,
Was it the waterfall of joy?
My gods, don't let me fail,
I'm gambling with my hope,
Please, let me have my toy.

The claws of life
Don't hurt me anymore,
Don't leave the ugly scars.
From eight to five
I'm working as a whore
Then drinking in the bars.

A Dialogue

My pastor said," Remember,
The Lord is only one for all,
He is not your daily handler,
Today, he helps another soul.

If you're pushed against the wall
With troubles on your shoulders,
He may decide to solve them all,
He's moved much bigger boulders.

Too much is on your plate?
There are no real friends?
Work on your gloomy fate,
God has two caring hands.

Today, you'll climb the wall,
Tomorrow, you may even fall,
Life is a turning lathe,
Don't lose your faith."

I said: "It sounds very good,
Though, hear me if you would,
I've seen them, mark my word,
On every corner of the world.
Too many clones were sold,
They look exactly as you, Lord."
Besides, I said after a pause,
"There are no helping elves,
God lends a hand to those
Who help themselves."

A Dollar Rules the World

We buy our precious time,
We sell our bearded prophets,
We never waste a shiny dime,
And quickly count our profits.

The green dollar is a god;
It reaps our daily praise,
And like a lightning rod
Unveils its terrifying face.

Our god does not forgive,
It's not his public trade,
I am afraid, he will receive
From us a passing grade.

We did not have to guess,
We knew.
A dollar rules the world,
In spite of our lifelong mess,
We are still silent at the pew,
The pastor doesn't say a word.

A Deadly Fight

A grisly night
Stuck behind a day,
A deadly fight
Is soon on the way,
A bloody war
Is waiting at my door.

A chicken got its head cut off,
And hurried to a ditch himself,
God struggled to divide a loaf
Among the hungry twelve.

We open our friendly doors,
Expect the Prince of Peace,
But face the goddamn wars,
I wonder, if the choice is His?

He offered us His sacred wine,
As blood, I wonder His or mine?
He offered us a gate to Bliss,
I'm confident, these wars are His.

Why do we trust
A self-inflicted god?
Why do we trust
A soul-dead angel?
I checked with my iPod,
I'd rather trust a stranger.

I trust,
We're condemned to lose,
I trust,
We have the will to choose
And dump all organized religions
That treat us
As gullible and gutless pigeons.

I'm old and wise, I'm eighty plus,
I kicked them out of my bus.

A Cold December

I always had a knack
For getting in a pickle,
I lost a fortune in the Jack,
Yet saved a worthless nickel.

I'm eternally adrift at sea
And keenly breathing fire
On everyone in Tennessee,
Who preaches to the choir.

I'd rather be under than above,
It's easier to hate than love.
Heaven can't wait.
The stairway needs guardrails
For me to reach the gate,
If I ascend, then Satan fails.

I didn't realign myself
With the stairway to bliss,
I have committed
An intellectual high treason,
I left my self-inflicted prison,
Then pulled my Bible
From the shelf
And tuned myself for the abyss.

The fallen angel died,
Christ came to wake me up,
He didn't pass by me that cup,
Therefore, I'll be crucified,
But won't be resurrected.

Christ said, "I didn't die,
I simply acted."

I still reluctantly remember,
That nights are for the stars,
That days are for the sun,
That dusks are for the bars,
But only a cold December
Remembers those who've gone.

A Chaotic Verse

I admire my image
In a glass of wine,
It's like a pilgrimage
Into this soul of mine.

My curiosity enters the world
Such no one has heard or seen,
My soul and body pledge to follow.
Ever since the doctors cut the cord,
I regularly taste a strange cuisine,
Easy to chew, but hard to swallow.

They didn't see us as their friends
When our tortured souls returned,
Cannon fodder in that dire war
Killed the innocence of youths
And took us to our lives' dead-ends,
Where our pasts were burned
Off cuts here locked behind the door
To isolate their lies from our truths.

We simply lost, we didn't fail to win,
We keep returning into our skin,
Like pages into book covers.
Like hiding secret lovers.
I weave a dark chaotic verse,
Most thoughts are not connected,
I'm creating a self-serving universe,
Where even the gods will be perfected.

A Brutal Tempest

A brutal tempest is in vain
And hides our gentle sun,
It pounds us with heavy rain
On our never-ending run.

We run our tiresome lives
Between a fire and ice,
Then fly into safe havens
As doves or sinful ravens.

We drink a luscious wine
Then cross the line,
We savor our apple pie
Then fade and die,
We see the rays of light
Then start that flight.

We boost esprit de corps,
They disappear in war.
Some trust, a better life begun,
I say they'll never see our sun.

At dawn,
We're devils in disguise,
At dusk,
We're angels in the skies.

A Book of Wasted Days

The living corpses
Of dying heroes,
Eternal sources
Of perpetual zeros.

Our daily life is war,
Brave guards, no winners,
Graveyards of dreamers
All behind the door.

We win a battle,
We lose a war,
We drown in a puddle
And slyly beg for more.

I write my book
Of wasted days,
Another look,
Another face,
Another page,
Another outrage.

The scars and bloody noses,
The footprints of lost loves,
Sharp as the thorns of roses,
Don't touch without gloves.

The frozen tears
Run down my face,
The past still bothers.
I dream of peers
I can't embrace.
Where are you, brothers?

Across the Fire

There is no breeze
In my soul's fire,
I learn to step aside,
So, I could cease
My soul's desire,
Its other cooler side.

I learn my soul,
It's black and white,
It's seldom rosy,
It's often gray,
Through a keyhole,
It's a dark day
Or a light night,
It's hardly cozy,
On my solitary way.

I wouldn't waste a speck of blood,
Even a snowflake during a snowfall
Or drops of murky water in the flood
To save my sinister imaginary soul.

I didn't want to see it anymore,
Dumped wreckage hit the floor.
It is a bitter truth of my existence,
I march alone a lifelong distance.

Across a Lifeless Field

The wall of worries,
A few loose bricks,
The fading stories,
The burning wicks.

The bitter autumn tears
Stream by a windshield
Of my red pick-up truck,
The country road veers
Across the lifeless field,
I'm tracing my good luck.

Nostalgic waterfalls
Of endless sorrows
Over my daily strolls
Toward new tomorrows.

I lost a bosom friend,
I lost my loving girl,
These rhymes evoke
My thankful elation.
I hold a bird in hand,
I let the vultures swirl
Into a wreaking havoc
Of my self-flagellation.

I took my own advice,
And crawled into a bed
To close my teary eyes
And act as if I'm dead.

Accordion

A rather shaggy veteran of war,
He hides a pain behind a smile,
He walks for us an extra mile,
Plays an accordion at our door.

His songs could melt the snow,
I still remember that melodic flow,
A passerby would drop a penny,
I was too young, don't blame me.

As cannon fodder with a bayonet,
He fought. I learned my alphabet.
The days of amity no one forgets,
The Kremlin's looming silhouette,
The polished medals on his chest
Suggested, wars were laid to rest.

Hello, new life knocks on my door,
Those memories still living here,
Farewell, ferocious flames of war,
Years passed, the skies are clear.

I mended wounds some time ago,
I left those gloomy native shores,
These days, I listen to accordions,
Blindfolded by fresh medals glow,
Digesting melodies of other wars.

Above the Valleys and the Hills

Above the valleys and the hills
Our ladies act as caring caters,
They come along as airy sylphs,
But later they become dictators.

We live to know our troubled ways,
Grace under pressure in the chase,
The masquerade of enigmatic fights,
We lose the days, we win the nights.

I never run away from dangers,
I sing my granny's tender lullaby,
"Life's full of foes and strangers,
But never let it pass you by!"

Life is a constant thirst,
Please, mark my word,
The trials come first,
The lessons afterward.

Above the Sins of Fallen Angels

My verses run across the pages
Without fear, misery or pain,
They fly over abandoned stages
Washed by the strings of rain.

The chill of a wintry flow
Falls on the hollow seats,
A tablecloth of snow
Hides our wasted pleas.

Forgotten shipwrecks cry,
And mourn for drowned strangers,
The leaky clouds calmly fly
Above the sins of fallen angels.

There are no angels in the sky,
Our life's a contest of attrition,
It's what we do and this is why,
We stretch our earthly mission.

The blind will always lead the blind,
Their verdicts are already signed,
They're inmates without guards,
They'll live eternally in our hearts.

Above the Red Clay Roofs

I left my comfy life of unanimity
To medicines in daily boxes,
I left the loneliness of my infinity
To rabbits terrified by foxes.

I'm following blue birds
Along the concrete city fiords,
Above the red clay roofs,
Containing our lies and truths,
Looking like red wine stains
Among the avenues and lanes.

I wouldn't help the gods
To send their lightning rods,
I wouldn't help the devil
To reach a sainthood level.

My thumb pushes the scale,
I need to see the day of light
Behind the leaded clouds,
I'd like to see the rainbow arches
Behind the timid gray.
I fled my self-perpetrated jail
Of never-ending doubts,
To hear the brassy marches.

There's no money in my purse
To buy or cease a falling knife,
There's no time to pen my verse,
There's no time to live my life.

Above My Roof

Above my roof, above a cobweb of new twigs,
The moon hangs like a chicken with no wings,
Blind owls are watching chipmunks in the grass,
A bat invited me to eat mosquitoes. I will pass,
I'm extremely honored, but as a real epicure,
I cultivated a fine taste and try to keep it pure.

I watch a rabbit running from the dog,
The hare is jumping like a damn frog,
I loathe these furry rats, the squirrels,
I aim my gun; they jump into the holes,
I see the glowing eyes of a young bobcat,
A cousin of a tiger, though chews the fat.

I didn't mention a white-tailed deer,
Who is too young thus has no fear,
When I give him an oatmeal cookie,
He eats and thinks I'm really spooky.

I didn't mention yet my neighbors,
From me they won't get any favors,
They're petty thieves and nonbelievers,
They steal my firewood like beavers,
They come to dance on my backyard,
Their son plays waltzes in his kazoo,
I need a well-trained bodyguard,
I'm in danger – it is a real zoo.

Above My Nervous Walks

I was habitually breastfed,
By ever-loving mother-sky,
The fast-red-tailed hawks
Above my nervous walks
Taught me to soar and fly.
I tried, but failed and bled,
Even the clouds didn't cry.

My friend, my horse,
My morning breeze,
Don't be too coarse,
Run gently, please.

I'm tired; I'm cold,
I'm wired, I'm old,
I spur; I pull the reins,
I run my longest mile
Over my futile gains
Toward the final trial.

I hate the changes,
I never greet the springs,
I shy away from strangers,
I'm a man without wings.

The Eternal Freeze

I walk along the aisle,
I long for my own seat,
Next to a growing pile
Of verses incomplete.

My place under the sun,
My own, the only one,
I crave to rest in peace
Inside the eternal freeze.

Black rain,
Red roofs,
Above the noise of pain,
Over the stomping hoofs.

I hear four horsemen,
I see their faded colors,
It is the rainbow of despair,
It is my ultimate nightmare.

I finally enjoy my peace
Under a slab of granite,
Inside of the eternal freeze
Of my melancholic planet.

Above a Garden of My Soul

As trumpets of aggression,
As tender violins of peace,
Betrayal, love and passion
Brought our farewell kiss.

A mirror on the wall of life
Reflects our wretched years,
The endless vicious strife
Among our laughs and tears.

In search of the beginning
We march toward the end,
Deaths close our vain living,
Only the lucky ones ascend.

An angel hovers in the sky
Above the garden of my soul,
He sees a teardrop in my eye,
A gracious witness of my fall.

After extensive sugarcoating,
The worthless entered bliss,
Only the garbage floating,
The worthy sank in the abyss.

About Life Which Passes by

I struggled from afar,
From wrong to right,
My winking guiding star
Unveiled a chilling sight:
The lightning left a scar
On the descending night.

I couldn't swim or walk,
I couldn't ascend and fly,
I wasted many sunny days,
I am a badly wounded hawk,
My castles faded from the sky,
There is no future to embrace.

My wisdom that I wasted,
Descends on me again
Experienced and altered,
I see the cultivated land,
And whistle a familiar refrain
Comforting and warmhearted.

It's easier to ascend,
It's harder to descend,
It's easier to touch the sky;
It's harder to disdain or cry
About life which passes by
And sneers at my goodbye.

I see the land of gold,
Under the angels' sky.

Why am I cold?
Why do I sigh?

I am too old to reach the gate,
My body drags the yoke of fate.
God never counted the years,
I sailed the rivers of my tears.

A Prisoner of Love

There are no bounds,
Our unfolded souls
Make silent rounds
On scorching coals.

You never tried to praise
Morality of murky scripts,
A tempting sparkly glaze
Still dances on your lips,
I kiss your stunning face,
I touch your tender hips,
Your eager body sways
In my avid, fiery embrace.

I'm your hostage,
A detainee in jail,
A prisoner of love,
"Dear, set me free,
Delay the carnage,
I promise not to fail,
I'll reach the edge
Of the eternal glee.
I promise not to fail,
I'll reach the edge
Of the eternal glee."

Not everything has gone,
Two tiny candles burning,
I'm not the only one
Whose love is yearning.

A sunny isle of hope
Reflected in your eyes,
I climb its shiny slope,
Like Satan in disguise.

A Prism Breaks Light

A house smells like fresh paint,
Bright flowers in every room,
The host reminds me of a saint,
Once resurrected from his tomb.

Farewell, boys went off to war,
Goodbye, children have gone,
Even the angels shut the door,
No one will see another dawn.

We often heard His voice,
We rarely touched His face.
I'm one of those brave boys
Recounting those ugly days.

The land is for the fallen,
The sky is for the living,
Only the ragweed pollen
Consoles the unforgiving.

Our dreams are darkest,
Before they're wholly black,
Our failures are the hardest
Before the ending smack.

A prism breaks a ray of light
Into the seven mortal sins,
Into a shattered darkness.

Then innocence begins.

A Predestined Tomb

Along my birthday piety
The ages blind my eyes,
Evoke a civilized society,
I can no longer recognize.

In vain, I hanker for a friend
With one Achilles heel or two,
I want to love her to the end,
Until the skies are never blue.

As saber-rattling quiets down,
"Make love not war"
Won't come too soon,
I throw away my judge's gown
And stroll across this afternoon.

A street palm reader outlined
My strange and tragic fate,
My self-defeating lethal bind
Of sins before the golden gate.

I will be trampled to death
By grateful and cheery crowds
That trusted me to take them
Into the blinding sunny clouds.

They'll descend into a gloom
That used to comfort me,
For bliss is a predestined tomb
Without a fairytale of glee.

A Precious Trophy

Days make me wise and older,
Nights wake up youth in me,
It's all in the eye of the beholder,
Remaining in that vivid glee.

My love is playing hide and seek
Like a delightful coquette
With my revealed desires,
I run from bright to bleak,
Like talents, undiscovered yet,
Like stars reflected in quagmires.

Two candles burning on the table,
Champagne's freezing on the ice,
Looks like a grand finale fable,
Or rather a disaster in disguise.

A trembling, fragile flame
Casts shadows on her face,
She is a gorgeous portrait
In a golden frame,
She is a precious trophy
Kept in a showcase.

I'm writing something on a side,
Hiding my schizophrenic fears,
My antiquated mythopoetic ride
Takes me to a waterfall of tears.

My girlfriend won't be back.
Dead-end or a cul-de-sac?

A Poor Composer

The vultures circle in the sky,
Their shadows iron battlefields,
The fallen brothers never cry,
The fighting never yields.

I watched my feisty past,
Revisited my gory youth,
Only the lies forever last,
I waved goodbye to truth.

Insufferable nightmares
Loom closer,
A house of faceless cards
Won't hide me anymore,
Life's like a poor composer,
Who writes a military march
For a so-called final war.

A fallen brother finds his home
In a flag-covered coffin
Through Andrews Aerodrome,
I've seen it all too often.

My country gained a fatal flaw,
That lastly wrecked its will,
The rulers sodomize the law
And solely appreciate the thrill.

It is a Castle in the Air

It is a foggy castle in the air,
Obscure mirage of an affair,
Please, give me back my life,
You're a stranger, not a wife.

I'll do as Paul Gauguin,
I need to find my Tahiti,
I am not a committed fan
Of life in my lackluster city.

I wouldn't run from guilt,
I run from dread and wilt;
I never blamed a mirror
For wrinkles on my face;
Today, I see much clearer,
Great pressure over grace.

The dance of our life is on,
We see the flashing light,
We hear the saxophone;
You beg me, hold me tight,
Pour honey on my heart,
Love isn't a forbidden art.

It Had Been Said

It had been said,
You have a quest,
Just move ahead,
Don't be my guest.

I am tired of your song,
I am tired of your speech,
Just watch your tongue
And, please, don't preach.

Ask "how do you do?"
Don't change my life,
I know what to do,
I know what I like.

I am tired of your stabs,
I am never in the loop,
I am among the baobabs,
I am foreign in this group.

Don't climb the boulders,
Don't climb too high,
Get off my shoulders,
Unfurl your wings and fly.

It had been said,
You have a quest,
Just move ahead,
Don't be my guest.

Into My Doubts

Between the oaks,
Under the clouds,
The autumn soaks
Into my doubts.

A bristly lightning-saber
Parted the blanket-night,
My fate set by the cradle,
Not by the passing light.

The end of tour:
I leave you all,
I leave the hell,
I finally am sure
I hear the toll,
I see the bell.

I am a lonely clever oak
Hit by the lightning-blade,
I peeled off my leafy cloak,
Erased my homely shade.

Late autumn grieves
Over its fallen leaves;
Even a tea rose mourns
Over its broken thorns.

The tears of olden pines
Cast ambers in the sand,
I use them in these lines,
I flaunt them on a strand.

The diamonds of thoughts,
The emeralds of calmness,
The dreams of floating boats
Sink in the sea of numbness.

Innocent Pontificating

Today, you take,
Tomorrow, give away,
It's not a modern flake,
There is no other way.

Today, you are a guest,
A host tomorrow,
It is your daily quest,
You either lend or borrow.

Be kind and always tip,
A dollar in their pocket
Will make a faster trip
Into the higher bracket.

Don't follow penny-pinching trends,
Be nice to strangers and to friends.
Don't ever spit into a water well,
Someday, you will need to drink
Before you slide to Hell.

Indian Summer

My life's Indian summer
Tries to delay my death;
I cannot hold a hummer,
Don't hold your breath.

No valor in the crowd,
No one thinks out loud.
In avalanche on doubts,
In hurricane of thoughts,
I hear those futile shouts
In silence of their throats.

I've seen this movie
Too many times before,
I shall remain yours, truly,
Please, never ask for more.

I went through thick and thin
Into the end no one desired,
I didn't commit a mortal sin,
My executioners misfired.

My sentence wasn't signed,
I lived. Death sadly whined.

In the Maze

Life often burns,
We heal the scars,
The globe still turns
Under the falling stars.

When darkness falls,
I meander in the maze
Between the quiet walls
Without love and praise.

New day rebuilds
Our burned bridges
Across the battlefields
Above the shiny ridges.

I call most of the shots;
Make some decisions;
Loosen too many knots,
And boost blurred visions.

Reality erased another fable,
I have to choose my venue:
Consuming dinner at the table
Or being on the menu.

In Spite of Warnings

A few auxiliary warnings
Run avenues and streets;
I am gambling at the Ritz.
Until worn-out mornings.

My pastors hate my glee:
They block my honey well,
They chain and push me
Toward the existential hell.

I am forced to love sunrise,
I am forced to love sunset,
I am born just once not twice,
It is a chance to place my bet.

Life is a film in slow motion;
Just let me cross the ocean,
And I will solve the riddle,
And I will thread the needle,
And I will hold the final straw
In our terrific life-river flow.

Goddess Justice is unnerved:
The ancient heroic fables
Will not be served
On our green gambling tables
Before the devastating fears;
Unless our courage stops
The waterfalls of cheers,
The rivers of teardrops.

I will clarify my hustler's drive:
I only learned the signs of life
And hid that secret envelope.
It was a calculated ploy,
A duty only, not a joy:
No one can ever find
What was never lost;
Oh, never mind,
The case is closed

In spite of Our Pain

My temper's tinderbox
Is waiting for the spark,
I came to check the locks,
Today, I'm not a happy lark.

Our days of goodness
Felt like a real bliss,
Forgive my rudeness,
Let's hug and kiss.

A fearless albatross,
Predicts the winter drifts,
I'm a prophet of my loss,
I failed to heed our gifts.

A sweaty chill lives
In my loving heart
As a perpetual rain,
The falling leaves
Set out loves apart
In spite of our pain.

I dreamed about you
Before we ever met,
Let's start anew,
It's easier to say "yes",
Than your Russian "net".

I am Talking to Myself

I hear my melodies and tunes,
I read my never written verses,
I am so full of fire and fumes
Why do I hate the controversies?

I'd rather run and stumble,
Than crawl and crumble;
Most think, that I am mad,
What if I am a step ahead
And lead if someone follows
To freedom from the gallows?

Don't cast before a swine your pearls,
Don't check the teeth of a gift horse,
Don't argue with a fool; it is a curse,
Follow your vision, stay the course.

Straight from the horse's mouth:
Don't ever listen to these clowns,
I've met some fakers for an hour,
They try to build the Babel tower.

I'm Ready to Forgive

Forgive me, I have sinned,
The stars still blink and glow,
And birds hide from the wind,
My footprints melt the snow.

My guilt breeds sighs
And sweaty fears,
I never close my eyes,
But gladly change the gears.

I leave behind
My empty bottle,
I'm sober, wise and kind
Like a smart Alek Aristotle.

I dig into my mind,
It's my turn to give,
The verdict walks aside,
And I'm learning to forgive.

Our selfish, greedy lives
As old as Eve and Adam,
In both castles and the dives
Life is a constant bedlam.

Some learn to take,
Some learn to give,
I know truth from fake,
I'm ready to forgive.

In my heart's holy room,
You're a bride; I'm a groom,
First love won't ever die,
Let's never say goodbye.

Another spring is right on track,
I laugh and sing, my life is back.

If Only It Were True

Some wrap their bodies in a sari,
Some soar into the foggy blue,
Some raise the dust over safari;
We're happy. If only it were true.
The grapes that grew in pain
Morph into a great champagne.

Banality is what I think,
Reality is a missing link,
I am up to my neck in ruckus,
I am worshiping fat Bacchus,
A luscious wine is my reward,
Trust me and mark my word.

A thin long thread
From our hazy past
Connects our lives,
Our daily bread,
Our nightly fast,
Our wicked tribes.

First love, I had my only chance,
I missed your promised dance;
Life dealt from a loaded deck,
I flipped a quarter in the skies,
I guessed and closed my eyes,
It landed badly. I am still a wreck.

The head, the tails,
The tails, the head,
My intuition fails,
I rarely get ahead.

I'm Married, but…

My French is a petty baggage,
I whispered, mon petite chou,
My sugar or my little cabbage,
She said, "I really like you, too."

Je suis Marie, mais…
I'm married, but…
I heard to my dismay,
It was a comma, not a dot.

Your place or mine?
I heard this in some movie scenes;
It is polite among the old marines.
I never failed to try,
The end must justify the means.

She was a curious French tourist,
I waved and stopped a yellow cab,
I'm not and haven't been a purist,
I chose the Plaza and ran the tab.

A charming hour of bliss,
The rising tides of heat,
The passion of a farewell kiss,
The joy of guilt-free bonus treat.

I said, "au revoir, my friend,"
And fondly kissed her hand,
I wished her wealth and peace.
Does such a fling have any merit?
My answer is,
Bad girls are already married.

I'm Good Luck Bound

I'm braced for a sunny day,
For the whispers of the sea,
I hope to find my own way
Within the maze of filigree.

My dreamy river dried away,
And trembled like a netted fish,
I tried to walk on feet of clay
Out of such an awful dish.

My loneliness was learned,
My punishment was earned
By every fearless albatross,
That missed the Holy Cross.

I must see happiness today,
As death may come tomorrow,
I must discover my own way
Across the sea of sorrow.

I have to thread the needle,
I have to find friends to keep,
I have to solve the riddle
And force my foes to weep.

I'll see the bastion of hope,
I'll reach the higher ground,
I'll climb the steepest slope,
I'm good luck bound…

A Prism of Pain

Some truths, some lies,
We pray as Mathew asks,
For those,
Who closed their eyes,
For those,
Without happy masks.

We ditched
The primal word
And lived in vain.
We try to ditch
The prism of pain
Through which
We view the world.

An angel of forgiveness,
The savior of our souls,
Forever pure and sinless,
Had never taken our calls.

A minus met a plus,
It didn't take too long
Before the lightning rods
Created animals in us.
To know right from wrong,
We have invented gods
Of second chances,
We walked our extra mile
Across a greener grass
Beyond the fences.
Death waited for a while.

A treacherous terrain
Under the waving twigs,
Absorbs a weeping rain,
Forgiving our intrigues.
Even in our saintly camouflage,
We couldn't sneak into eternity
Of bliss.

A sight of a well-timed mirage
Showed a bridge to the abyss.
Nobody has two final breaths,
No one can have two deaths,
Our escape into the dying arts
Gives us a fragile hope to live
In memories of living hearts.

Creative Powers of Distractions

Dark shadows crowded the room,
I played here as a child,
Even the efforts of a brand-new broom
Won't resurrect all those who were exiled,
Tortured, hung, killed or sent to prison
Without any jurors, crime or reason.

The time ran, flew, but never walked,
While I was staying still and numb,
Yet, once upon a time life talked,
The days of make-believe will come.
I waited for a mischievous and wicked elf,
Instead, the bloody history reversed itself.

The creative powers of distractions
And foggy legacy of revolutions
Still knocking on each door
And bitterly demanding actions,
Passing half-baked solutions
Including yet another war.

Today, the power of the powerless,
The heartless terror
Abruptly changing our souls
For now, and forever,
Casting vile shadows on the walls.

They crossed these rooms,
Connecting our births with deaths,
From primal cries to modest tombs,
From wombs to final breaths.

Convergence

The days of a ruling terror
Brought me into a fight,
I am not a standard-bearer,
But learned to see a light.

I am shot and left for dead,
I am hanging on a thread
Along the miracles of life.
I'll return with vengeance,
I'll be ready for the strife;
Gents, start your engines.

Another up and down day,
So outwardly sad,
All talk, no action.
My friends already say
That I am definitely mad,
Maybe beyond retraction.

I am climbing to perfection
Between my endless rivals;
The winds are howling
Amid the wicked trees,
Anticipating our arrivals
Into the Promised Land
Of our biblical trustees.

It looks like a doubtless
Divergence
Of the Big Bang and deity
Convergence.

C'est la Guerre

I try to glue, in vain,
A pair of broken candles,
My memory still handles
Two lovers on the train.

The history repeats
As rainbows' arches
At times, it marches
To railroads' beats.

We shared a single night,
Not from the war nightmare,
There was no peace in sight,
You whispered, "C'est la guerre."

We learned to wait,
It seemed forever,
We knew it was our fate,
It was our destinies' endeavor.

One night of love and kindness,
Fell into the bluff and blindness.
One-night affair, two dreams,
Deux Mers or just two streams?

I never quit, I'm eighty-seven,
I trust we'll meet in heaven.

Bonfires of Red Sunsets

Bonfires of red sunsets
Grins through the pines,
A pretty melancholic set,
Pierced by the fiery lines.

A theatre of the deadly game,
The boys get wounds and scars,
The generals get blame or fame,
After the bloodstained daily farce.

The tragedy of war is varnished,
The gleam of medals tarnished,
The veterans meet once a year,
We hug and drink or drop a tear.

Not every one of us
Lives reasonably well,
Some went to paradise,
Some dwell in Hell.

Bizarre geography of Loves

In my upbringing
Of a mute obedience,
I learned
The filigree of flirting,
The short but tedious,
At times, mood-swinging
Rituals of courting.

I learned
Bizarre geography of loves,
The oddity of long affairs:
The science of their bluffs,
The silence of their glares.
The vivid memory of nights,
The unforgiving fiery fights,
Derailed geometry of wrath,
Deserted bitterness of math.

When days were rough,
No lucky wood to knock,
I never climbed the wall,
I didn't think about love,
I only stopped the clock,
And let the castles fall.

It was a jolly ride
Among my peers,
All pledges died
Along these years.

Blurred Lines

Life's a sheer phantasmagoria
From the abyss to paradise,
From carnage to euphoria
From battles to a compromise.

First, someone gives the word,
The Big Bang forms our world.
Blurred lines of deadened feelings
Hide warning signs of quiet killings.
My Lord, help me through the day
Then change the rules of our play.

Life's heartbeat scarcely trails
My verses' streams of rhymes,
Wheels knocking on the rails,
I scream and bite my tongue,
Trying to gain on wasted times,
Naively splitting right and wrong.

Our compassion hardly handles
The bitter tears of our mothers,
The absence of fallen brothers.
The blown-out birthday candles,
Gave me a wish to learn enough
About a rivalry of hate and love.

Canary in the Mine

Last night, a total outrage,
The miners pared my wings,
Then locked me in the cage
And hung it on the strings.

I didn't cry, I didn't whine
As a canary in the mine.
In every mine of our lives,
Most go down; a few rise.

I hated noisy grinders
No one could ever fix,
I hated grimy miners,
I liked their shiny picks.

After they'd load the train,
I'd see through dusty haze
The silent gaze of an insane
On every blackened face.

The sirens go off, shift ends,
They take the dusty elevator,
Lunchboxes in their hands,
And "See you later, alligator."

I couldn't see their rules,
I lost my reading glasses,
I rarely smelled the fumes,
I've never sensed the gases.

I was forever kept inside,
Endlessly bored and tired,
I never sang, only complied,
Today, at 65, I finally retired.

Cards Will be Dealt

My guarding angels
Hover in the skies,
I even close my eyes
But never see that far.

No patience anymore,
I walk across banalities,
Then wipe the floor
From soiled trivialities.

After a sudden nightfall
The world looks gray,
Under the starry shawl
Nobody is above the fray.

I'll wait until next spring,
I'll learn to cry or dance
Among the frantic herds.
I'll take another chance,
I'll learn to fly and sing
Among the cheery birds.

The snow starts to melt,
Here comes the spring,
Cards will be dealt,
What will they bring?

Callous Choices

I touched the edge of our universe,
But only reached the end of numbness,
This voyage rearranged my verse
To share enlightenment with dumbness.

I'll forever think in lingua franca,
I pulled and tore my native roots,
Only a sentimental Casablanca
Still greets my pirouetting boots.

I stand in front of callous choices,
My quandaries are far from ending,
I hear the wingless angels' voices,
"You have to think of your ascending.
It's written, there's no village
Accepting its homegrown prophets.
While, nobody condemns a pillage
And grab the waterfalls of profits."

The anxious heads of my inspired pens,
Are eager to reinvent another senior god
To solve the mystery of eggs and hens,
And pierce the dragon with a lightning rod.

I won't surrender to a new dogmatic faith,
I won't abandon freedoms of my mind,
My tarnished conscience wants to bathe
In muddy waters of god's inferior mankind.

But I Come Back

I love the travel stickers
On our luggage cases.
Retired pleasure seekers
Appreciate exotic places.

No one is waiting,
But I come back
Into my guiltless youth,
Into my puppy dating,
Into my hunting knack,
Into that spotless truth.

Rain washes late September,
I shoot some birds at dawn,
My pointer quick and slender,
Anxiously veering on the lawn.

I walk along a morning breeze,
The friendly melodies of nature
And quiet whisper of the trees
Bring all my ills into their cure.

Then why do I always go back
Into the urban jungle of concrete,
Into my dilapidated gloomy shack,
Where ends would never meet,
Where life hangs on the rack
Or marches to its own heartbeat?

I lived on borrowed time, but didn't reimburse the lender.

Acknowledgements

I am deeply grateful to Judith Broadbent
for her skilled professional guidance
And generous stewardship;
For her unyielding yet wise editing,
Which allows me enough room
to exercise my whims.

To Kate Broadbent for her help with
Selecting and suggesting poems.

To Anna Dikalova for her kind ideas
and a firm belief in my success.

To a great artist, Mary Anne Capeci,
who graciously allowed me to use
her painting for the cover of this book.

To all my friends for their continuous
And gently expressed motivations.

Thank y'all, PZ

Printed in the United States
by Baker & Taylor Publisher Services